Force

for

Christ

Force
for
Christ

The First Ten Years
of the Northern Branch
of the Christian
Police Association

Christian Focus Publications Ltd

Published by
Christian Focus Publications Ltd

© 1990 Christian Focus Publications

ISBN 1 871 676 07 X

Christian Focus Publications is a
non-denominational publishing house. The
views expressed in our books are those of the
authors.

Contents

Introduction

When knowledge came to hand of the intent to have this book, covering the activities of the Northern Branch Christian Police Association, published and, at the behest of those involved that I should write an introduction, it offered me much pleasure. My wife Margaret, my daughter Rhoda, and I have had close associations with the Northern Branch since its formation in 1980. Having been a member of CPA since May 1954, when I joined the Royal Ulster Constabulary, the intervening years have provided precious memories, with colleagues of like mind, of journeys at home and throughout the United Kingdom, all testifying to God's saving grace and keeping power.

In retrospect, we have convincing evidence that the Christian Police Association was, in its origin, a movement of the Holy Spirit to reach the hearts of such a noble body of men and women, that they might be won for Christ. Those Spirit- motivated of all who worked for God throughout the years have witnessed the hand of the Lord in the lives of many in the Force, and also a rich overflow to others who remain to this day, whilst many, of blessed memory, are now with the Lord.

The Coming Day will declare it all, but appropriately we make reference to the 1980 Inauguration of the Northern Branch held at Police Headquarters, Inverness. It was a very special weekend; the Lord was present, and Chief Inspector Murdo MacLeod's testimony in this book relives for us what God has done. There were also Mhairi MacIntosh and Margaret Mackenzie, with others, in the following years, all of whose names are written in the Book of Life.

Altogether, my personal involvement with the work of the Northern Branch, and the fellowship experienced, have left indelible impressions with me which remain to this day. The remembrance also of so many gifted servants of the Lord who have ministered the Word of God, which was greatly appreciated and resulted in the spiritual edification of the people of God, is no doubt reflected within the contents of this book.

The work of the Christian Police Association goes on apace. We are all part of it, serving the Lord with joy.

In much earlier years, the Association to its credit also had a worthy interest in the social needs of the members and, although time and circumstances may have altered the emphasis, the uniting of believers and the extension of the Kingdom of God remains our prime spiritual pursuit.

In a very personal way, as former President of the Northern Ireland Branch, present member of CPA Council since 1975 and a past Chairman of that Council, I would say, Be of good cheer! The Lord is on our side. This little book will no doubt have a unique place in the Association's library and should be purchased by a wide section of the reading public, within and without the Force, as its existence is broadcast by members.

We wish it God-speed!

Tom Davison

Ex Chief Inspector

Royal Ulster Constabulary

Preface

I am so glad that the Lord gave me an early interest in Tape Recording, for as soon as He applied His saving grace to my sinful life I found myself applying His gift of recording technology to the taping of gospel messages and sermons, and it is from such recordings that the addresses which form the major part of this publication have been transcribed.

What a God of providence we have! During the several weeks that I have been compiling the contents of this book, and as memories spanning a ten year period have been brought to mind while engaged in typing the draft manuscript, it has been so clear that God's mysterious providence has been manifestly evident in the history of our Northern Branch CPA; so before you read this little book, I would ask you to stop for a moment to ponder on the various providential factors which had to take place before you could read it. Here are some starting points for you to consider, but bear in mind that they by no means form an exhaustive list.

First of all, Miss Catherine Gurney, the founder of the CPA movement, had to be at the right place (or was it the wrong place?) at the right time to enable her to stop a particular police officer for directions, and he had to respond quizzingly in the way that he did about her little gospel tract concerning his soul.

A century later, a young Christian police officer at the opposite end of the country, David Beatty, had to be given, by God, a very active interest in the Christian Police Association to persuade him that Northern Constabulary should have a Branch. Sufficient Christian police officers with similar interest in having a Branch formed had to be stationed in or around the Inverness and Dingwall areas to provide the nucleus required for Branch Inauguration.

The same God of providence ensured that our dear friends the Davison family from Northern Ireland would attend the Inaugural meeting, would stay with the MacLeod family for the purpose of Murdo receiving God's salvation through Tom's ministry and of course, ten years later, relating his experience in this publication. In total contrast, the testimony of Mrs Margaret Mackenzie, Dingwall, bears witness to God strangely preventing her from attending a CPA meeting, but again with the same glorious purpose in view - the salvation of her eternal soul; in this case, as is so often the way, through the reading of His precious Word in the solitude and quietness of her home.

Another is that the now not so youthful writer of this article, with little interest in godly matters, had to be led to a fascination with tape recorders, had to be converted and then made to re-apply his use of the invention from the recording of Scottish Dance Music to more spiritually profitable recording material. In this matter I must personally confess that amid the hustle and bustle, a characteristic of CPA Anniversary weekends, it was always a last-minute effort to gather the equipment together and set it up to record the principal speakers at the Anniversary meetings, and I would therefore thank God for applying sub-conscious promptings which thwarted my tendency to slothfulness and thereby ensured that the addresses of His faithful servants were preserved over the years for this special publication.

What about the mystery of that 1985 Anniversary

address by Rev Dr Robert McGhee of Falkirk? Robert came with his message carefully prepared for the occasion as is characteristic of that servant of God, but God prompted him to preach on a totally different text that evening. Why? The God of providence alone knows the reason but it was interesting to later learn that a young woman was saved at that meeting!

One final providential point is most worthy of mention. At an evening fellowship meeting during the ninth Anniversary weekend, and following the reading of a particular portion of God's Word, a publisher and brother in the Lord Jesus Christ was convinced that he should make an offer to publish a book to commemorate the first ten years of the Northern Branch of the Christian Police Association. At that particular time, unknown to him, there had already been typed the first of the ten addresses of the principal speakers, for it was my desire to try to produce a modest typewritten manuscript of the ten principal speakers' addresses before the tenth Anniversary in 1990 as a memorabilia of the Branch. God works in a mysterious way His wonders to perform!

Why concentrate, though, on providential happenings? Well, I believe that if there is one area of modern-day Christianity that is deficient it is attempting to understand God's providence. Even a cursory reading of the godly Puritan writers will clearly illustrate a profound perception and a commensurate evangelistic zeal related to that perception of God's providence, as well as highlighting our late twentieth century scant interest. We believe that God has blessed our Northern Branch CPA over these past years, in ways which would be inexplicable were it not for His own providential dealings with us. We confidently send forth this book in the same glorious knowledge that He will providentially use it to His glory despite the inherent weaknesses of the human contribution.

It would be impossible to acknowledge every individual person who has supported Northern Branch since its formation for there are many behind-the-scene workers, including our many sisters in Christ who so often have to bear what appear to be the menial tasks in the ongoing work for the Lord. Then, not least but rather especially, there are those who plead our cause in prayer and whose deserved recognition must wait until the King Himself rewards accordingly. Nevertheless, two names do most certainly merit inclusion in this Preface - former Constable David R. Beatty, the first Branch Secretary, and Sergeant William J Murray, his successor and present Branch Secretary. These men shine as lights in the annals of our Branch, and we pray that the Lord will continue to bless their commitment to His service.

It would be remiss to leave readers with the impression that everything associated with the Northern Branch has been a bed of roses. The true believer in Christ with a sound Bible knowledge would be immediately suspicious of such an account and the unbelieving reader would be left with a not uncommon modern-day false impression of what the Christian life is all about. I am reminded of the true words of a godly minister who said, 'God promises to eternally save the Christian from the awfulness of hell but there is nothing in the Word of God that guarantees the Christian that in this life he will escape the assassin's bullet or the ravages of illness or disease.' As an

Association and as individual members of that Association, we are aware that we may not be spared the waters, rivers and fires of life but are conscious of the fact that, in treading these mysterious pathways, we shall experience the presence of One who will accompany us and who has provided advance comfort by saying, 'When you pass through the waters, I will be with you; and through the rivers, they shall not overflow you. When you walk through the fire, you shall not be burned, nor shall the flame scorch you. For I am the Lord your God, the Holy One of Israel, your Saviour' (Isaiah 43: 2, 3).

We have had our disappointments. There have been personal backslidings which Satan attempts to keep us in remembrance of; there have been attacks on our Branch's evangelical and reformed stance; there have been the critical as well as the complimentary comments on our Branch Newsletter articles, but what can be faithfully assigned to print is that overall these ten years have been happy years, years of glorious fellowship; in particular the Anniversary weekends, where new friendships are commonly forged and old friendships renewed, have almost been a foretaste of what in our limited knowledge we believe heaven to be like.

I would warmly invite the reader to taste in print some of the rich food that our Branch feasted on during its existence in The First Ten Years.

O taste and see that God is good!
David B Topping
Founder Member

The Christian Police Association - its history

'What! Do you think a policeman has a soul?' That remark was made over a hundred years ago by a young Constable on the beat to Miss Catherine Gurney, a lady whose life was dedicated to the service of Jesus Christ her Saviour, and who had a burden in her heart for the police officers of her day. Through her prayers and untiring effort, and undeterred by the unpopularity of the police in those days, Miss Gurney took a great interest in the force and was instrumental in the formation of what initially was called The International Christian Police Association.

The heart-searching reply of that young police officer who was so obviously unaware of the danger of neglecting his eternal soul, stirred Catherine Gurney to encourage Christian fellowship and witnessing for Christ within the police force. This Christian work amongst the members of the police force was sanctioned by many senior officers who concurred with her published aim to place before the men of the service a high ideal of life and service made possible through the redeeming grace of the Lord Jesus Christ and the indwelling power of the Holy Spirit.

What about this gracious woman herself, a woman obviously led by God to see the institution of a movement which for the next century at least would be dedicated to bringing the gospel of the Son of God to thousands of police officers and their families? Catherine was the youngest daughter of Joseph Gurney, a member of the firm of short-hand writers serving the Houses of Parliament and the Old Bailey. A woman of great knowledge and ability, she would most likely have gained distinction in various fields of secular service, but God confronted her with the claims of Jesus Christ, His beloved Son, whom she accepted as her personal Saviour while still a young lady.

Catherine first served among the poor and needy at Wandsworth near her home where she commenced a Men's Bible Class. It was around this time that her interest in the police developed.

Miss Gurney longed for a place where police, off duty, could relax away from the atmosphere and pressures of their work. Following a visit to a young officer in hospital who had been badly injured in the course of his duty, and who had expressed a desire to get away from the police Section House atmosphere to read or write letters in quietness and in more relaxed surroundings, Catherine Gurney was spurred on to rent an office in London, WC1. The Lord's leading became evident, however, when a large house near Charing Cross, overlooking the River Thames, came up for sale at a very reasonable price. In the providence of God, No 1 Adelphi Terrace, London, WC2 became the Headquarters of the International Christian Police Association and remained so until the Second World War. Throughout the years many police officers and their families spent off-duty hours in this home and , not surprisingly, many were introduced to the Lord Jesus Christ as their personal Saviour and the Friend that sticketh closer than a brother.

Catherine Gurney's work in connection with the welfare of police officers and their families went from strength to strength, and within a few years Convalescent Homes were opened in Sussex and at

Harrogate, Yorkshire. Again, more than just physical recoveries were experienced as many, whilst recuperating from illness, responded to the glorious Gospel of the Saviour.

Catherine Gurney's vision for the Association extended world-wide, and, through her travels and correspondence, Branches were established in America, Canada, South Africa and Europe. The Association was indeed truly international in nature; but for various reasons, and to avoid confusion with another organisation, it became known in later years as the Christian Police Association or CPA for short.

CPA has flourished since those early days of prayerful beginnings, and like the woman in Scripture with the alabaster jar of ointment, although admittedly to a more limited extent, Catherine Gurney's name is still mentioned amongst succeeding generations who enjoy fellowship under the auspices of an Association which the Lord saw fit to establish through one of His faithful servants.

The Christian Police Association
Its Aims, Members And Basis Of Faith

AIMS

To promote and foster the fellowship of Christian Police Officers in that unity which is enjoyed by those who are born again by the Spirit of God;

to demonstrate this relationship to God in a concern for righteousness both on and off duty;

to obey Christ in proclaiming His Gospel, especially to members of the Police Service that they might be brought to know Him personally.

FULL MEMBERSHIP:

This is open to Police Officers, former Police Officers, and their wives, who know the Lord Jesus Christ as their personal Saviour and who are in agreement with the Aims of the Association.

ASSOCIATE MEMBERSHIP:

This is open to interested Christians in other walks of life, who are in full agreement with the CPA Basis of Faith, and who are willing to support the work of the movement.

BASIS OF FAITH:

1. The Unity of the Godhead and the Trinity of the Persons therein;
2. The Incarnation of the Son of God, His Virgin Birth, His Sinless Life, His work of Substitutionary Atonement for sinners, His Resurrection and Ascension, His present Mediatorial Intercession and Reign and His future Personal Return;
3. The work of the Holy Spirit in Regeneration, Conversion and Sanctification;
4. The Divine and complete Inspiration, Authority

Force for Christ

and Sufficiency of the Holy Scriptures as
originally given;
5. The utter Depravity of Human Nature in
consequence of the Fall;
6. The justification of the sinner by Grace through
Faith in Christ alone;
7. The Immortality of the Soul, the Resurrection of
the body, the Judgment of the world by our Lord
Jesus Christ, with the eternal Blessedness of the
Righteous and the eternal Condemnation of the
Wicked;
8. The obligation resting on all those who name the
Name of Christ, to afford evidence of their
discipleship by a life of obedience to His
commands.

18

Personal Reflections

I am most grateful for the opportunity afforded me in being invited to contribute to a book celebrating the tenth Anniversary of Northern Branch CPA. I do hope that what is contained in these paragraphs may be inspiring and, above all, God-glorifying.

Eternity will reveal, no doubt, a much wider and fuller picture of the Lord's hand in providence. I realise that I am only one 'little part' of a plan which God interwove to bring about His work in this Branch of the Christian Police Association. It is nevertheless a rather strange matter, and I have often marvelled at it, that the first Branch Secretary of the Northern CPA was born and bred in Northumbria and yet, as a child, was nurtured with a desire for the Scottish Highlands and fed upon a child's romantic picture of his father's former Highland Regiment.

Privileged to have been converted at the age of twelve, I recall the year 1970 when, at the age of fifteen I sat with my late father, the Rev. J Rex Beatty, within the Police Headquarters of the Durham Constabulary at Aykley Heads, Durham. The occasion was the Inauguration of the Durham Constabulary Branch of CPA. There were about 100 people gathered at this memorable venue, and in the distance I viewed the platform party. There was the recently appointed General Secretary of CPA, the Rev. George Roberts (who retired from this position in February 1989). I could see Inspector Robin Oake who later, much later, was to attend the Inaugural Meeting of the Northern Branch CPA, and who is now Chief Constable of the Isle of Man Constabulary. I also have a vague recollection of a small group of police officers meeting periodically in our home for prayer and fellowship, but like most youngsters, uninitiated in the police environment, I stood somewhat in awe of this group of specialised people.

This all made a deep impression, for you have to remember that this was the close of the 'swinging sixties', and so, what an inspiration it was to a young Christian teenager to see a small group of fine Christian police officers with such pioneering and fearless zeal, so unashamed of their faith in their place of work! Here were men and women willing to identify with Christ outside the confines of their denominations and in the nitty-gritty of their work environment. It was at that Inaugural Meeting in Durham that the Lord placed a longing and yearning in my heart to follow such footsteps one day, wherever He would place me when I entered the police service, for such was my desire.

A year later I entered the Durham Constabulary as a Police Cadet and eighteen months after that I joined my family, who had moved to the Highlands. I later joined the former Inverness-shire Constabulary, which in 1975 was absorbed into the amalgamated Northern Constabulary. It is impossible to convey in a few words the intense feelings of loneliness and at times despair that seemed to mock and isolate me as a young single police cadet, and later as a fully fledged police officer while stationed in some isolated postings. Any dream which God may have given me seemed threatened by the sense of total vulnerability. However, it was during these years that the Lord gave me this little thought, 'When is an outpost not an outpost? When there is "One who sticketh closer than a brother." '

It was while I was stationed at Aviemore that CPA, at national level, became a source of tremendous blessing and encouragement. The General Secretary at that time, Rev. George Roberts, and Detective Sergeant George Smith, then Branch Secretary of Edinburgh Christian Police Association, used to write what became treasured *Epistles of Encouragement*. Through membership of CPA, the On and Off Duty magazine, and later the fellowship of Christian police officers in neighbouring forces, the burden of isolation was alleviated.

After Aviemore I spent a short time in the City of Glasgow Police, but within a year found myself back in the Highlands and once again a police officer, this time in Inverness. God was sovereign in all these movements and all were extremely important in relation to the formation of the Northern Branch CPA. The period in Glasgow had been a maturing and solemnising experience. It had also been a wonderful encouragement from a CPA point of view, for the City of Glasgow Branch of CPA (now Strathclyde Branch) was very active at that time and I was privileged to learn from a widening family of Christian police officers. The City of Glasgow Branch organised house meetings to co-ordinate with shifts, and their outreach extended to the Force Training School where new recruits would be encouraged to identify with CPA fellowship. It was here, a little green with envy, that I compared the fellowship offered these Glasgow recruits with my own isolated past in the north, something I prayed would change if the Lord guided me back to Inverness.

As I have mentioned, within a year I was back in the north - city policing was not for me! Although still very young, I had now grown to love the police service and thoroughly enjoyed my work in the Northern Constabulary. Desire within me was strong for the formation of a Northern Branch CPA, and in March 1976 a circular was posted from my home in Inverness to local Ministers and several CPA contacts. A prayer meeting was to be established for the formation of CPA in Northern Constabulary. While there were only two of us who met at that first meeting, we nevertheless claimed the promise of Matthew 18:20 and straightaway agreed the venue for our next meeting. By the second meeting, prayer objectives had been answered - the Chief Constable had given permission 'in principle' to the establishment of a force CPA Branch, should we at some future date be in a position to meet the numbers required for a Branch Inauguration. By mid-1976 our Circulars were being sent to various parts of the force area and to the Scottish Police College, where new contacts were made. Those early days were thrilling ones and the sun seemed to shine upon our fellowship.

Picture a small group of young police recruits on their second-year training at the Scottish Police College, Tulliallan, Kincardine-on-Forth, the National Training School for all Scottish police officers, all of us with hair close-cropped and gathered in the small room beneath the stage next to the barber's 'salon', our studies over for the evening. An instructor at the College opens the meeting in prayer, while a Detective Sergeant from Lothian and Borders Police has travelled thirty miles or so to come and encourage us in the Word and to speak to some of the colleagues who shared the dormitories with us. There are other young police officers, male and female, from various Scottish forces also bowed in prayer. After the meeting we return to our dormitories encouraged, and unashamed to witness for our Lord. The Lord gives us strength to kneel by our beds at the eve of the day. Colleagues in the dormitories seem eager to ask questions and enquire about the lives of the Christians in the respective sections and quarters dotted about the College. Meanwhile, back at force there were now colleagues praying for us during our training course at Tulliallan. Interest in the Christian Police Association was growing.

There was, however, to be a gap - or an apparent gap from a human point of view - in the structured organisation of a potential Northern Branch CPA from Summer 1976 until August 1979. The Christian Police Officers were still scattered all over the force area (Northern is the largest 'geographically' in Great Britain). During part of this period, I left the force and spent a period in Bible College, little thinking that I would ever return to the police service. However, that was not to be, and soon the Lord had me back in the service and posted to the remote Island of Barra, and later Benbecula, a total contrast from theological training! Behind the scenes, I was later to discover, the Lord was quickening and preparing many Christians throughout the force for CPA Branch Inauguration.

In 1979 a lovely event occurred in my life when I was married to my dear wife Ishbel. In the Lord's good time He had brought us together in a truly unique way, and now I had a special helpmeet to share in the vision and work of CPA! After our marriage in Ishbel's native Skye, we were posted to Dingwall, Ross-shire, and around the Inverness and Dingwall areas we soon found that the Lord was drawing together a nucleus of Christian police officers and their families. What happened from then on was 'the Lord's doing and wondrous in our eyes'.

August 1979 saw the issue of CPA Circular No 8, and by this time the distribution extended to twenty-two people including recent recruits. Meetings were extended to three main areas of the force, with Dingwall area meetings organised by myself, Western Isles by Sergeant Norman Murray (now retired) and Inverness area by Sergeant David Topping (now Headquarters). Bi-monthly house meetings were held and prayer support encouraged.

About this time there was much correspondence with CPA Headquarters, Leicester, regarding the establishment of Northern Branch CPA. Despite staff shortages at CPA Headquarters at this time, Rev. George Roberts pulled out all the stops and worked tirelessly for the realisation of that vision of the formation of a Northern Branch CPA, so long prayed for throughout the many years of preparation.

On 4th September 1979 I wrote to the Chief Constable, on behalf of my colleagues in Northern CPA, reminding him of the earlier request in 1976 for permission to form a Branch, and seeking his renewed approval for an inaugural meeting to be held at Police Headquarters, Inverness in early 1980. On 25th September 1979, a memorandum was returned to me at my Station with the words 'Approved - Chief Constable.'

Between late September 1979 and Friday 7th March 1980, those involved in the pioneering work of CPA Northern Branch enjoyed halcyon days of unrestrained joy in preparing for that great event which finally brought the yearning of so many years to realisation.

THE INAUGURAL MEETING FRIDAY 7TH MARCH 1980

Words could not describe our feelings as we worshipped the Lord that special Inaugural evening at Police Headquarters, Inverness.

Out of the corner of my eye, I saw my father (who took me as a young lad to that first CPA Inaugural meeting in Durham), my family, my wife, friends with colleagues and families from all over the United Kingdom, including those dear friends from the Royal Ulster Constabulary - *all one in Christ Jesus*. So many who had helped, inspired, and encouraged me over the years, and without whose undergirding and unfailing influence there would have been no Branch of Northern CPA! As the many members of the new Branch were called to be upstanding for the prayer of Dedication of the Northern CPA, there stood at that meeting the one who was to succeed me as Branch Secretary two years afterwards, Detective Constable William J Murray from Lewis, another faithful pioneer. Almost 200 people crowded the Headquarters Hall for what will always be a most memorable occasion in my life, and I'm sure in the lives of all founder members of the Branch. The Inaugural weekend was also of course very special for Sergeant Murdo MacLeod (now Chief Inspector and Force Traffic Officer) for it was then that he came to know the Lord as His personal Saviour.

The first year was one in which the Lord was pleased to bless the Branch in a way that was simply of His doing. Quite a number of colleagues, hitherto unknown, requested information about the aims and witness of CPA. Others came to the Lord at this time.

Much prayer was required, and the early days were not without their opposition. As the Branch became known, so cynicism was experienced in some quarters. In my own Station, for example, the monthly Newsletter that was displayed on the noticeboard would continually disappear, until in the end we used Bostik! Prayer and Bostik can be effective!

The Chief Constable graciously allowed the use of Force facilities to print our monthly Newsletter and the use of Headquarters premises for our meetings. On one occasion in the early days, we printed a special magazine and distributed it to every officer in the force. Some of us may recall the enveloping with some amusement!

Force Open Day at Inverness presented us an opportunity as a Branch to display materials related to CPA and the gospel. Many members of the public attended these Open Days and many showed an interest in our Display Stand.

It was also a privilege on one occasion to be asked by the Chief Constable to be in attendance during a visit of the Moderator of the General Assembly of the Church of Scotland to Force Headquarters, and to meet with the Moderator. But perhaps for me, one of the most significant and fulfilling moments in that first year was when permission was granted to issue to every new recruit to the Force an information leaflet on the subject of the CPA. This offered fellowship, understanding and encouragement to Christian recruits, and provided information about CPA to the interested officers just enquiring about Christian matters.

THE FIRST ANNIVERSARY - MARCH 1981

By the first Anniversary, the Lord had prospered the work and blessed it beyond all our expectations, and on this occasion we were forced to move venue to the Inverness Town Hall because of the large number of people expected to attend - an expectation which was realised. Many more colleagues had come to know the Lord and many people from outside the service were showing an interest in the Branch.

MY FAREWELL

In October 1981 the Lord graciously renewed His call to me to the Christian Ministry and in particular the United Free Church of Scotland in Dounby, Orkney, where I was to serve as Missionary/Pastor for several years before entering the ordained Ministry in Aberdeen.

What a privilege it was to have a CPA mission in Orkney during my Pastorate there and to enjoy the continuance of the fellowship and the enrichment of Christian police fellowship while ministering the gospel!

Today, as this little book is published in connection with ten years of CPA Northern Branch, we look back with gratitude to God for the established work of the Christian Police Association and for the knowledge that the present Branch Secretary and members and friends have served faithfully and constantly to maintain that work and witness to Jesus Christ in the wide sphere in which He has placed them in Northern Scotland.

In closing, I would leave this Bible promise with you to take into the future years - 'Being confident of this very thing, that He which hath begun a good work in you will perform it until the Day of Jesus Christ' (Philippians 1:6).

May the Lord continue to bless the Northern Branch in the years ahead.

From one who is 'A Debtor'.

Rev. David R Beatty

First Branch Secretary

Northern Branch CPA

Now a Pastor to Northfield United Free Church of Scotland, Aberdeen.

Message by William J Murray
Branch Secretary, Northern Branch CPA, from 1982 - Present Date

In 1982 our first Branch Secretary and founder member David Beatty left the Police Service for full time Ministry. This brought a real sense of loss to members and friends in the Northern Branch. His departure was tempered only by our knowledge that he was acting in obedience to God's call, and that his work in establishing the Northern Constabulary Branch of the Christian Police Association had evidently been completed.

In those early days we had witnessed David's untiring devotion to the Cause of Christ as he forged ahead in the face of many adversities. We saw his determination as he laid the foundations of the Branch and sought to bring police officers and their families to a saving knowledge of Jesus Christ. David bore all his responsibilities with a warm and ready smile, and we have much reason to praise and worship God that his efforts were so richly blessed.

With the Branch rooted in the Doctrines of Scripture, and giving principal place to the proclamation of the Word of God, the succeeding years brought tremendous blessing in evangelistic outreach. Although clearly and absolutely subordinate in every respect to the reformed denominations of the Christian Church, the Christian Police Association stood in the strength of the Lord and matured through the inter-denominational membership of those police officers and friends who were truly born again of the Spirit of God. It became a joy and a privilege at our meetings to see the amalgamation of Christians from different denominational backgrounds coming together as one to praise and magnify the Lord. To this day it is so and is the source of much thanksgiving.

Over the years, the Branch has grown from a handful of members to a figure in excess of thirty police officers (5% of the force) who are truly born again and profess Christ as their Lord. In many cases, the wives of those police officers also profess the Lord, and combined with a significant number of Associate Members and faithful supporters, the Branch has continued to flourish and enjoy the Lord's blessing.

This can perhaps be best gauged on a spiritual level by anyone attending our Annual Meetings where the Lord has oftentimes used those means to His own glory in the conversion of souls. In recent years the venue for our Annual Meetings has had to be moved on two separate occasions to accommodate larger audiences, and at our most recent Anniversary Meeting in 1989, the number of people attending was in excess of 450. We do indeed praise God for the widespread support and encouragement we receive from throughout our force area.

The work of the Branch in terms of evangelism is directed to three main fronts. The first of these is personal contact in the work situation, secondly, tract publication and distribution, and thirdly, monthly ministry meetings. The first mentioned is extremely important and continues quietly and unobtrusively from day to day as the opportunities arise. The tract distribution, in the form of our Outreach magazine, extends to all police stations in the Northern

Constabulary, with many individual officers in personal receipt of our monthly issues. Our mailing list for Associate Members and friends outwith the police service is currently in excess of 100, and it is gratifying to learn from time to time that the message is appreciated and considered worthwhile. We are very well aware of our own limitations in this field but we are confident in the knowledge that the Lord will bless that which gives Him the glory and is in accordance with His own will. Our monthly meetings are usually held at centrally situated police stations and provide a gospel message together with a time for prayer and fellowship. Speakers are carefully selected on an inter-denominational basis in a way which reflects the diversity of membership in the Branch. Everyone is welcome and the Branch is greatly encouraged by the continuing interest and response of those who attend.

The wide distribution of Christian police officers throughout our vast geographical area makes it impossible for everyone to come together at fellowship meetings, but the very fact that those police officers are dispersed in this way is in the Lord's hand, and we trust that their influence and witness in their own communities will further advance the Cause of Christ and enhance the public service which they seek to provide.

Members of the Branch are often called upon at Christian gatherings to speak on the subject of CPA, and invariably the question is asked, 'How can anyone be a police officer and a Christian?' The response to this question lies at the heart of all that has been said so far, and in its simplest form can be answered by saying, 'How can anyone be a police officer *without*

31

being a Christian?' By being a Christian, the individual is better fortified to withstand and cope with the demands of work, and far from being a disadvantage or a contradiction, the Christian life is a supremely satisfying life-style and one which fully complements his or her professional role as a police officer. When Christ rules in the life of a person, whatever that person's profession may be, that life has a quality and an influence for good which permeates through personal circumstances and overflows into the work situation. The same is true of the Christian police officer.

In the police service of our day much is said about stress related illnesses which are attributed to traumatic and violent experiences at work. These experiences certainly do exist and Christian police officers, in common with their colleagues, are exposed to all their evil influences. Christian police officers, however, have an awareness of an ever-present recourse for such stress related factors - a ready access in Christ to the Throne of Grace - undeniably the best place to bring life's cares and worries as well as one's consciousness of sin. 'Come unto Me all ye that labour and are heavy laden and I will give you rest' (Matthew 11:28). The Christian police officer is therefore one who urgently and earnestly encourages colleagues to come to this place in prayer, for here alone can peace, security and strength be found wherewith to face all of life's traumatic experiences and stressful situations.

As we look forward to the future as an Association, we are conscious of the fact that hitherto has the Lord helped us. We therefore place our reliance and confidence for the years ahead upon the goodness of

God and not upon any achievement or merit of our own. We remain daily dependent upon the mercies of a Sovereign God and our desire is to serve Him in the place of His choosing. We are thankful to Him for the witness of CPA and we pray that in the decade to come we will continue to know His blessing and rejoice in His salvation.

Testimony by Northern Constabulary Traffic Officer - Chief Inspector Murdo MacLeod

A WEEKEND TO BE REMEMBERED

During the weekend of 7-10th March 1980, Mary, my wife, and I were privileged to have Chief Inspector Tom Davison of the Royal Ulster Constabulary, his wife Margaret and daughter Rhoda staying with us while they attended the Inauguration of the Northern Branch of the Christian Police Association.

At that time Tom travelled throughout the Province of Ulster in connection with his work. It was admirable that neither he nor his family complained about the troubles and dangers that they faced daily. Their Christian strength, their faith in Christ and the love of their Master's work and ways were an example for others to follow.

They did not themselves bring up the topic of the troubles in Ulster, but when asked about it they freely discussed the situation and related incidents of which they had personal experience. Stress has become a word in common use in police circles in recent years, but consider for a moment the greater reason for colleagues in Northern Ireland to suffer from stress.

Imagine being awakened by your wife in the early hours of the morning and being told that she heard a man running round the back of the house and that she suspects that it is a terrorist. Shortly afterwards you hear the person running to the front of the house; you immediately jump out of bed and, being unable to find your gun, you go outside unarmed to investigate, only to find that on this occasion it was a new milk delivery man! The tension eases but for a moment it was extremely stressful. Or imagine being cornered in a

34

cul-de-sac, with gunmen shooting at your party, until some hours later you are able, under the cover of darkness, to crawl on your belly across a field, through a fence and across a motorway. Christian members of the Royal Ulster Constabulary did not then and do not now want or need sympathy. What they do covet are the prayers of other Christians.

I am thankful to God for the stay of the Davison family in my home that weekend. It was the means used by God to bring me to put my trust in Jesus. Up until that time I had lived a morally upright life. I attended church very regularly. I did not, however, have a personal relationship with God. Yes, I read the Bible and I even prayed to Him. All my life I knew of the reality of a heaven to be gained and a hell to be shunned. It was only when Tom talked into the wee small hours of that Saturday morning, explaining the simplicity of salvation by careful use of the Scriptures clearly explained, that I was led as a child to see that I had a duty to respond to the invitations of the gospel.

THE INTERVENING YEARS

Since then my family and I have made many other friends among Royal Ulster Constabulary officers and their families, including the gospel singer and author Detective Constable Ben Forde. I would recommend Ben's three books, *Hope in Bomb City, Love in Bomb City* and *Faith in Bomb City*, to any who want to see the troubles of Ulster from a Christian viewpoint.

Mary, our two children, and I, along with my very good friend and colleague Chief Inspector David Topping, his wife Linda and their boys, have visited Northern Ireland and maintain a close contact with the friends there. David and Linda have been a tower of strength and encouragement to Mary and me during all these years and indeed in the years before my conversion when David sought to direct me on to the Christian pathway.

Many things have happened in the intervening ten years. I have seen God work in many wonderful ways. He has proved to me the truth of the Scripture in practical ways. I could relate many such instances but will limit myself to two. In doing so I am conscious that my motives may be seen as boastful but nothing could be further from the truth. My purpose is to encourage any Christian who feels inadequate to be of service to God. Be encouraged! He used me and He will use you. If I should want to boast then God tells me, 'let him who boasts, boast in the Lord.'

The first instance centres around 1 Corinthians 1:27: 'God chose the foolish things of the world to shame the wise; God chose the weak things of the world to shame the strong.' I have had the great privilege of being a foolish thing or weak thing in the hands of God as He has used me to lead others to Christ. One such occasion was when I was asked by a friend to speak to a man I had not previously known and who was not a Christian. He admitted that he wished to give his life to the Lord. I spoke to him only briefly, drawing his attention to the words spoken by the apostle Paul to the Philippian jailer: 'Believe in the Lord Jesus Christ and you will be saved.' The Spirit of God performed a great work in that man's life, because these words burned in his mind until he came to trust in Christ as his personal Saviour.

The second instance centres on Philippians 4: 13: 'I can do all things through Christ Jesus who gives me strength.' On an occasion when I was taking up new duties I was concerned over whether or not I would be able to deal adequately with things of which I had no previous experience. Before going to work that morning, the verse above quoted formed part of my Bible reading. I knew that God had spoken to me and that with His help I could undertake my new tasks with confidence. That can be the Christian's encouragement each day if we trust in the Lord with all our heart and lean not on our own understanding. In all our ways acknowledge Him and He will make our paths straight.

There have been many disappointments in the last ten years, mainly ones of my own making. Disappointment at not having been a better witness for Christ. Disappointment at having often failed to speak to others, including relatives, friends and colleagues about their need to have a personal relationship with Christ. I have disappointed the Christ who gave His life for me.

AN OPPORTUNITY TO BE GRASPED

I would ask all who read this testimony to examine their standing before God, who is not only a God of love but is also a holy God who demands that justice is done. Reader, do not be offended, because what I ask you to do, I demand the same of myself.

There is no one righteous, not even one, the Bible tells us. It also tells us that because of the righteousness of God, sin must be punished. The love of God is seen in His giving His only Son to suffer for our sins in His death on the Cross of Calvary.

In return God demands that we accept a gift, namely to come to Him, confessing our sins and turning from them. It requires us to put Christ first in our lives and serve Him. Do you usually refuse gifts? I am sure not! Then, why refuse this one? It is a gift that has everlasting effects. Each one of us would want, maybe even expect, to get to heaven after our death. If our confidence is in anything except in Christ it is a false hope. Christ Himself said that 'except a man be born again, he cannot see the kingdom of God.'

At a seminar for Senior Officers in this force, an officer during his presentation was speaking about a free service that his area was offering to the public in relation to crime prevention surveys. He said that he could not understand why a free offer was not being more widely accepted. Here is a greater offer that is yet rejected by many. The reason why these free offers are so often refused may be very simple. Is it not that people do not realise their need? The Prodigal Son would never have returned to his father's house unless he had become aware of his need: 'When he came to his senses ....' Have you come to realise your need of a Saviour? Have you come to your senses? The Prodigal Son did one other thing. He arose and went to his father. Will you not accept the free offer of the gospel? Arise and go to God in faith!

Maybe some who read this consider that the Bible is not relevant today. Be assured that it is not only relevant but it meets *every* need of today. God says of Himself that He is the same yesterday, today and forever. Science, rather than disproving the Bible as many would have us believe, actually proves the truth of it with many new discoveries.

For those in whom God works by the Holy Spirit, salvation is made very easy. It has to be, because it is the same offer that goes out to those who are of high intelligence as to those who are of low intelligence. It goes to the fit and strong and to the weak and disabled who may be able to do very little for themselves. All can, however, trust in the sacrifice of Calvary.

Salvation is free to you and me, but think of what it cost Jesus Christ. As He thought of what He was to suffer we are told that His sweat was like drops of blood falling to the ground. He knew the real meaning of stress! Imagine the agony of being nailed by your hands and feet to a cross. He endured that for us if we put our trust in Him.

If you are not a believer, will you not come to Christ without further delay? Now is the accepted time, now is the day of salvation is the Lord's message for you.

What is the alternative? While the answer to that question is not palatable it is fact. It is damnation! It is to be cast into a place that was not originally prepared for man but for the devil and his angels. It is a place too awful to contemplate.

During the last decade the Northern Constabulary has seen a number of young officers die. Each death is a warning to us about our own end. Each open grave reminds us that one day, if the Lord does not return soon, others will spectate as our remains are lowered into the ground. How urgent is the need for us to make preparation, and make our calling and election sure! God is no respecter of persons.

No doubt the decade now commenced will see similar tragic events, and who can tell but that you or I might be one of the central characters involved in some tragic circumstances. One thing is certain, that, after death we will face the Judgment.

Some of my colleagues will consider my comments to be narrow minded. Some would even say they do not believe what is said and will disregard them as if

39

they did not apply to them. Such was the reaction of one experienced officer. To dismiss the matter without examining the evidence may seem a strange reaction from one who is daily seeking evidence to prove criminal cases! To all of a similar mind I would recommend the book *Who Moved the Stone* written by an American lawyer who set out to try to disprove the Bible, and in the process was convinced of its truth.

Reader, how is it with you? Are you ready to stand before the Greatest Judge of all? By the grace of God I have an advocate in Christ Jesus. He is waiting to be gracious to you as He was to me.

Testimony by Mhairi MacKintosh, Parks Farm Cottages, Inverness

When did you become a Christian, Mhairi? These were words that rang in my ears on the 20th March 1982 as I was passenger in a car travelling on the A9 road between Dornoch and Inverness. How could I avoid answering this question? Could I jump out of a car travelling at sixty miles per hour? Never! I wasn't ready. Ready for what, you may ask? Ready to die, ready to meet God!

Why was I on that car journey with Tom and Margaret Davison from Northern Ireland, people I had never met before? Oh, I did enjoy being at the CPA Northern Branch Anniversary meeting in Inverness the previous evening, but why did David and Linda Topping ask me to go to the CPA Rally in Dornoch, and why, yes indeed, why did I go? Why did David ask me to travel with Tom and Margaret and why was I now faced with this awkward question? I know the answers to these questions now but at that time I was in a hotspot.

I did feel awkward but had to face up to the fact that I was not a Christian, and I can tell you that is not an easy admission when you are surrounded by Christians. A discussion began, and many points of the gospel of the Lord Jesus Christ were talked over, till I remember reaching the point where I said that if Christ came back to earth I would stand up on His side. Tom Davison told me that I had to take that step there and then and put faith into action, believing that Jesus died for me. He quoted John 3:16 substituting the word *whosoever* with my name, *Mhairi:* 'For God so loved the world that He gave His only begotten Son that *whosoever (that's Mhairi)* believeth on Him should not perish but have everlasting life.' I realised at that point that Jesus did die for me personally, and if I had been the only sinner in the world He would still have died that cruel death for me. There and then I accepted Jesus as my Saviour. Here I was only a few miles further down that same A9 road but now in a saved state where I was ready if Christ should call me home.

Arriving back at Inverness I just could not wait to tell Linda that I was now a Christian. I thank God for Linda and David and for Tom and Margaret Davison who were used by the Lord to draw me into His kingdom.

The Christian life is an exciting life but it is not an easy life - we are not promised skies of blue every day but we do have a wonderful promise from the second last book in the Bible, Jude 24, 25, which I will leave for you to take the time to go and look up.

Testimony by Mrs Margaret Mackenzie, Dingwall

When I was asked to write a few lines for this CPA tenth Anniversary book my first reaction was that I could not, but after consideration I then began to feel that no matter how difficult and unworthy I felt, I should keep before my mind that *Worthy is the Lamb*.

In March 1981, not directly associated with the Christian Police Association but during the weekend of the CPA Northern Branch Anniversary meetings, I came to trust in the Saviour for time and eternity.

I attended the Friday evening Anniversary meeting which I do not really remember much about now. I had been a seeking soul for some time but, on reflection, I now see that I was trying to work out my own salvation. I was so very disappointed on the Saturday evening that I would not be able to get to the CPA Rally meeting, but God is sovereign and His purposes, while so often unfathomable to our limited understanding, are yet excellent and perfect. I was confined to home that evening and while alone in my sitting-room I picked up my Bible and started reading in Matthew Chapter 7. When I came to verses 7 and 8 the words spoke to me as never before and, through the Holy Spirit, I came to realise that these words were sure and certain to my sin-laden soul. 'Ask and it shall be given you; seek, and ye shall find; knock, and it shall be opened unto you: For every one that asketh receiveth; and he that seeketh findeth; and to him that knocketh it shall be opened.'

At this time I was also reading a book, *The Memoirs and Remains of Robert Murray M'Cheyne* (a godly Scottish servant of the gospel who ministered last century and whose biography referred to has been reprinted by the Banner of Truth Trust). The part that I was reading was a letter from M'Cheyne, dated March 20th 1840, to a soul whom he had never seen but whose case had been laid before him by a friend. The whole letter spoke to me so clearly, but I will pick one or two parts that encouraged and helped me in particular at that time.

M'Cheyne writes: 'The poison of sin is through and through your whole heart but Christ has been lifted up on the Cross that you may look and live. Now, do not look so long and so harassingly at your own heart and feelings ..... You were shapen in iniquity and the whole of your natural life has been spent in sin ..... Look to Him and live. You need no preparation, you need no endeavours, you need no duties, you need no strivings. You only need to look and live. *For one look at yourself take ten looks at Christ.*'

I will close this little word of testimony with another part from M'Cheyne's letter, which refers to Christ's offer of salvation, and I would ask the readers of this book, whoever they may be and in whatever circumstances of life this finds them, to realise that this gospel offer is extended to them also. 'Whosoever will, let him take of the Water of Life freely' (Revelation 22:17) - the last invitation in the Bible and the freest ..... Anyone that pleases may take this glorious way of salvation.'

Reader, how is it with your soul? Have you taken of that precious Water of Life? Drink and live!

1980

Inaugural Meeting Address
Rev George Roberts, General Secretary

He is altogether lovely
(Song of Solomon 5 v 16)

No doubt many of you have been wondering how a little fellow like me could get in amongst these giants behind me. Ten years ago Robin (Robin Oake, who is now Chief Constable of Isle of Man Police) and I met together in London, and we heard God's voice that day. Like my colleague, it was not a pathway that I would have chosen, but I am glad that I listened to God's voice. These ten years have been years of great fulfilment in the service of our Lord and Saviour Jesus Christ.

The late Duncan Campbell often said that if a young man wanted to pay court to a young lady he would have to learn the Gaelic, for, he said, there are seven different words for love in the Gaelic language. The apostles had a similar problem when they came to describe their relationship with the Lord Jesus Christ. When they came to express the mercy of God in Christ Jesus they often ran out of language. Paul in seeking to describe the divine ability says that He is able to do exceedingly abundantly above ..., then he runs out of language. Peter, in trying to describe the joy that comes to the believer in the midst of trial says that we rejoice with joy unspeakable and full of glory. In the Song of Solomon the maiden is trying to describe her beloved and she says that he is altogether lovely. The

Song of Solomon pictures the relationship between Christ and His church.

We are here this evening because we have discovered that Jesus Christ is altogether lovely. We have found an attraction *in His words*. Remember when the Pharisees sent officers to arrest our Lord Jesus Christ. The officers came back to those who had sent them and their witness was: 'Never man spake like this Man.' There is in His words a certainty; I am the Light of the world, I am the Bread of Life, I am the Resurrection and the Life, whosoever liveth and believeth on Me shall never die.

We, in our doubts and in our confusion, sometimes when we are fearful, find an attractiveness in this certainty of Christ's words because of their simplicity. When we read the gospels, our Lord Jesus Christ takes His illustrations from the birds, from the flowers and from the seasons. If we look at His words we discover that they are simple so that the meanest intelligence can grasp what He has to say. There was something about their moral excellency, there was a clarity about His teaching. Roy (Roy Logie from Strathclyde Police, one of the visiting delegates at the Inaugural Meeting) was talking about values. When we come for instance to the Sermon on the Mount we get clear instruction on our values. Another attraction of His words is their timelessness. If I opened up this meeting for testimony, many, many people could refer to occasions when the words of our Lord came to them with a timelessness which is far beyond tomorrow's newspaper. There is an attraction in His words.

There was an attraction about *His works*, what He did. Remember that simple but sublime statement, 'He went about doing good.' We see Him at the well, at the graveside, by the sickbed, with the young, always doing good. He transformed human experience at every level. Remember the man who said, 'This I know, once I was blind, now I can see'. Ever think about that woman who had been bowed down for many years, of that transformation that came about in that home, because the Lord Jesus went about doing good.

There was an attractiveness in His words and in His works but oh, there's an attraction in *His personal glory* - who He is! First, He is God's prophet. Now a prophet speaks as the mouthpiece of God and with the authority of God. Jesus Christ is God's final word to this world. Second, He is God's Priest! A priest's function was to offer sacrifices. Ah! He has made a full, perfect and sufficient sacrifice and satisfaction for sin. He offered Himself a sacrifice for sin. I believe in the substitutionary atonement. My guilt and despair, Jesus took on Him there - Calvary covers it all. The function of a priest was to offer sacrifice. Another function of a priest was to make intercession. Oh, tonight, He is altogether lovely because He is at God's right hand interceding for me. He is my priest to offer sacrifice, to make intercession and to represent me before God. Third, He is God's King. God hath highly exalted Him, given Him a name that is above every name, that at the name of Jesus every knee shall bow. He shall reign for ever and ever. Jesus Christ is Lord.

There was an attraction in His words, in His works, in His personal glory. Ah! the attraction of *His death*! In John 3 there is the reference to the occasion in Israel's history when they had sinned. The instruction was given that a brazen serpent be erected, and those that looked to that serpent would be healed.

The Cross brings to us a reminder of rebellion and sin, but it also brings to us the assurance that our sins can be forgiven. In one of the psalms, we hear the Psalmist shouting: 'There is forgiveness with Thee.' Oh, it is a glad, glorious and triumphant message that there is forgiveness with God. I often think of that illustration in Bunyan's Pilgrim's Progress. When the traveller came to the foot of the Cross, the burden rolled from off his back and disappeared. Then the traveller gave three leaps for joy. I sometimes wonder what would happen if someone in our church, realising the glorious salvation that God has provided, followed the pilgrim's example and gave three leaps for joy. I think sometimes the deacons would ask them to leave. The pilgrim gave three leaps for joy and he cried, *'Blessed Cross, blessed sepulchre, blessed rather be the One who suffered there and died for me.'*

I say to you as one who has known His sovereign grace and mercy that He is altogether lovely. I say to you with one of the Covenanters of old, 'What ails you at Jesus?' Will you not respond to His invitation? Will you not come tonight and prove that He is altogether lovely? Amen!

1981

Rev George Roberts, General Secretary of CPA

Is Thy God Able?

One of the things which Ministers and Policemen have in common is that very often we are called upon to answer questions! People will come to us with questions that perplex and confuse them, particularly at times of danger and disaster. Then they ask, 'Does God care?' Side by side with that question we have the question that was asked of Daniel, 'Is the God whom you serve able to deliver?' Someone has said that circumstances are like a feather bed - if you are on top of them you are comfortable - if you are under the circumstances you are smothered! And that is true. This is the challenge I want to bring to you this evening - to face the question that the king asked and to answer that question from the experience of God's people and from the Word of God. Daniel was in the den of lions and I can see the king making his way to that den. He had had a very bad night with no supper the night before, he had not slept a wink and he shouted this question into the pit where Daniel was. I wonder sometimes was he surprised when he got an answer? Is thy God able? In those circumstances of extreme danger the answer is an immediate, 'Yes.' Daniel's life had been at stake but in answer to the king's question there is an immediate 'Yes.'

Why was Daniel able to respond so quickly? I want you to notice first of all that he made no attempt to adjust his actions to suit his circumstances. When the king's decree was issued he was absolutely clear about his duty. There had been a point in his life when he purposed in his heart that he would not defile himself (Daniel 1: 8). Here was a man in a position of authority who had subjected his life to the demands of Almighty God. There was no question of compromise, there was no question of expediency, because he trusted that whatever happened God was sovereign in the affairs of men. Daniel was able to answer immediately because there was no thought of compromise! Thus we read that he knelt and prayed as he did aforetime. He prayed to God for revelation, to make him faithful and as Ben (Ben Forde) has been illustrating to us, he prayed for his enemies.

I want to bring you to another question. It is found in Psalm 78:19. It is the question of a disobedient disciple: 'Can God furnish a table in the wilderness?' The children of Israel in obedience to God's command had left Egypt, crossed the Red Sea and were going to the Promised Land. But they lost their way. When we cease from following the Lord, when we turn aside from Him, this question inevitably comes up: 'Can God provide?' The answer to that question is in God's Word. The question was provoked by a desire to go back to the land of Egypt. At the heart of this incident there were three decisions. The people said, 'Let us go back'; Moses said, 'Let us stand still'; and God said, 'Go forward'. Can God furnish a table in the wilderness? This question is provoked by disobedience. But I believe from the Biblical record of God's dealing with men that the vessel that has been marred and broken can be made again. Am I speaking tonight to someone who has turned aside, whose life has become barren and empty, where your experience

is that of William Cowper when he said,
'Where is the blessedness I knew,
When first I saw the Lord,
Where is the soul refreshing view
of Jesus and His Word?'

Think of Paul on his last journey when a storm blew up; everybody's life was in extreme danger and disaster was imminent but the apostle Paul stood up and said, 'Be of good cheer for I believe God.' Is the God whom you serve able? The answer is, 'Yes.' And I will give you three reasons from Scripture.

He is able to save to the uttermost. In other words He is able to deliver completely from the guilt and power of sin. And why is He able to do that? He is able to do that because of who He is! He is the Son of God.

He is able to deliver not only because of who He is but also because of what He has done. It was my privilege a few weeks ago to stand in the Garden Tomb in Jerusalem and to look up to the place of a skull; to realise that on that hill the Lord of Glory took my sin and your sin and bore it on His own body on the tree. He is able to save to the uttermost. He is able to deliver completely because of who He is, what He has done and, thirdly, by His present ministry. As Ben (Forde) and Tom (Davison) and all the other police officers go on duty they have the assurance that Jesus Christ is praying for them. He lives forever to intercede for His people. He is able to save to the uttermost because of who He is, what He has done and His present ministry.

And there is more: He is able to keep that which I have committed to Him. My testimony is very similar to Ben's. In the Parish church in my home town, about seventeen miles from where Ben came

51

from, on a Sunday morning in 1948 I acknowledged the fact that I was a sinner in need of God's mercy and I committed my life to Him. Now I would have been incapable of any kind of victory over temptation if I had been dependant on my own character or ability but not only was He able to save me that morning but He was able to keep me. He is able to keep that which I have committed unto Him against that Day. He is able to do exceedingly abundantly above all that we could ask or think. God's salvation, may I say it reverently, is what one would expect from Him. It is complete, it is secure, it is supernatural!

If you ask me tonight or if you ask any of my colleagues on the platform this question, 'Is the God whom you serve able?' they will reply as I have, 'He is able to save'. That word salvation is the word deliverance. He is able to set us free from sin, He is able to keep us from sin and He is able to do for us way beyond our expectation. Is our God your God? I want you to say with the Scripture: 'This God is our God for ever and ever' (Psalm 48:14).

1982

Rev David Paterson, Free Church, Perth

Responsibility to witness (Ezekiel 3 v 17f.)

Now, this evening I want to read with you a few verses from Ezekiel chapter 3 and Revelation chapter 3. We read in Ezekiel chapter 3 v.17, *'Son of man I have made thee a watchman unto the house of Israel; therefore hear the word at My mouth and give them warning from Me. When I say unto the wicked, You shall surely die, and you give him not warning, nor speakest to warn the wicked from his wicked way, to save his life, the same wicked man shall die in his iniquity but his blood will I require at thy hand; yet if you warn the wicked and he turn not from his wickedness, nor from his wicked way, he shall die in his iniquity but you have delivered your soul. Again, when a righteous man doth turn from his righteousness and commit iniquity and I lay a stumbling block before him and he die, because you have not given him warning he shall die in his sin and his righteousness which he hath done shall not be remembered but his blood I will require at your hand; nevertheless if you warn the righteous man that the righteous sin not and he doth not sin, he is warned and also you have delivered your soul.'*

Also in Revelation 3 at verse 15 written to the church at Laodicea, *'I know your works that you are neither cold nor hot; I would that you were cold or hot; so then because you are lukewarm and neither cold nor hot, I will spew thee out of My mouth; because you say I am rich and increased with goods and have need of nothing, and you know not that you are wretched and miserable and poor and blind and naked, I counsel you to buy of Me gold tried in the fire that you mayest be rich; and white raiment that you mayest be clothed, that the shame of your nakedness do not appear; and anoint your eyes with eye salve that you may see. As many as I love I rebuke and chasten; be zealous therefore and repent. Behold, I stand at the door and knock; if any man hear My voice and open the door, I will come in to him and will sup with him and he with Me.'* Now may God bless to us the reading from His Word.

I am going to suggest this evening at the outset that the Bible is all about people and their God, and that the Christian Police Association is all about people and their God. Throughout the whole of this Book we learn how people meet God, how they walk with God, and learn how to obey and follow Him. We learn about their falls and their successes but constantly the one recurring theme is people and their God.

The Book of Ezekiel is also about a man and his God; a man who knew how to speak to his God and a man who knew how to listen to his God. You see, Ezekiel was a man who walked in powerful company. A few mornings ago while wondering what to use for this address, just as I was praying, I felt a verse of Scripture speaking to me. It was the 17th verse of Ezekiel chapter 3. It goes like this: 'Hear the word at my mouth and give them warning from me.' I turned to the book of Ezekiel and found where it was written and in looking through this chapter I felt that there was a message from God for us all. If this book is filled with the stories of people and their God, let's find out about it - to find out whether our Christianity is centred on our God and upon our relationships with

Him.

I found that the true messenger of God is in powerful company - directly from my text. 'Give them warning from Me.' God was speaking to him. God was not an experience of the past, that he could relate about something that happened years ago. His experience was up to date, he was in powerful company. And as I looked through the chapter, I found four things regarding this relationship he had with God. In verse 4 I found that he was under divine orders, 'Go, get thee to the house of Israel.' He had no option, and that's something we must learn about our dealings with God, we have no option. We think of what we want or what we'll do. When we walk with God we find there is nothing so comfortable and uncomfortable as to be under divine orders! It's uncomfortable when you're afraid of them, when they're difficult, but oh, the release and the peace of knowing that you're under them - that's deliverance!

The messenger of God is not only under divine orders but he is borne under divine power when he is in touch with God. How do I know that? In verse 14 he says, 'So the Spirit lifted me up.' God Almighty takes the poor and the needy and lifts them up when they have dealings with Him. This is not just a man who looks back and says that he knew God there and then. This is a man who looks up to heaven and says, 'I see God now, I feel God now, I'm going with God now.' You see the messenger! He is borne in divine power.

Then we see something else about the messenger of God in powerful company - we see that he is burdened by a divine responsibility. What does the truth here say? 'His blood will I require at your hand.' When we walk with God we must bear the burden of a divine responsibility. We become responsible for our neighbours, employees, our workmates, those who sit with us in church, our families, those that are lost. We become responsible, and the person who walks with God will become burdened with a divine responsibility. I speak to every Christian here in this meeting tonight, 'Are you burdened with a divine responsibility?'

In verse 22 we find something else about the man who walks with God. Listen to what it says, 'The hand of the Lord was upon me.' He was assured of a divine touch. Now this is not the touch that makes a man arrogant but the touch that makes a man feel small and yet at the same time makes him sense that God has something for him to do. That's the first thing that I noticed when I looked at the chapter that the true messenger of God is a man in powerful company. He is under divine orders, borne in divine power, burdened with a great responsibility and assured by a divine touch.

As I continued to study the chapter I found that not only was the true messenger of God in powerful company but I saw that the true message of God was divinely authentic: 'Hear the word at My mouth and tell them from Me.' In the chapter I saw three duties that are very important for a person who walks with God. Listen to them carefully. In verse 4 I read this: 'Go get thee to the house of Israel and *speak My words* unto them. Not just pray for them, speak them! Be vocal! And then in verse 10 there is a slightly different slant: 'Son of man, *all My words that I speak unto you receive*.' Not only My words but all My words. The person who walks with God not only has to hear God's words but all God's words. The words that deal with our private sins, our selfishness, our lack of Christian consistency. The person who walks with God and who is in contact with Him will receive the Word of God in two areas - one will be the area of the intellect where the Word of God will so to speak go through the ears. But not only is the man of God to hear the Word in his intellect and store it up but he has to hear it with all his heart in the throne of the personality, in the deepest part of his being so that it will be obeyed, loved and followed. Thirdly in verse 17 you read this, 'Hear the word at My mouth.' Hear My word, hear all My words and hear it at My mouth. God is saying: 'Hear it from Me personally.' Do you hear it from God personally?

Now there are five things about this message given to the prophet. It was a specific message; it was a personal message; it was a public message; it was a frightening message; it was a factual message. But it is for *you*, because God said, 'Hear the word at My mouth and give them warning from Me.' The message is for you tonight who are without Christ. There is one thing we do not find in the whole of the Bible - extra time for a sinner to repent. The true diagnosis of God is devastatingly simple. There are two things in it - you find it written in verse 18. Listen carefully: 'When I say unto the wicked, "You shall surely die", and you give him not warning, to warn the wicked from his wicked way,to save his life, the same wicked man shall die in his iniquity.' And then in verse 19, 'If you warn the wicked and he turn not from his wickedness he shall die in his iniquity if he turn not from his wicked way.'

There are two things here that God is pointing to in every person who is without Christ. First his iniquity and second his wicked way. Our iniquity is the inner source from which everything evil comes. Our wicked way is the outward expression, the things that we do, the things that we say, the things that we think. They come from the inner source and are the outward expression of a fatal disease. In the inner source, according to the Scriptures, we see the seat of man's rebellion against God, a part of our inner being that we cannot deal with ourselves. The wicked way is the evidence of our rebellion. Many people speak, and I have heard it on the television this week, of the violence of our day, but violence is only one of the outward expressions. Many people who live in sin of all kinds will speak against violence but they will not speak against their own darling sins, their own wicked ways. Why? Because of the seat of iniquity in us all.

If we are going to deal with God, God has got to deal with our iniquity at its source. The sickness of the spirit is our inability even when we try to live by conscience and the Word of God - we are unable to do it, but not only are we unable to do it, we refuse to do it. The Bible is about people who have had their inner source dealt with by God, who have had their wicked ways changed by God. Our problem lies both in our inability because of sin and in our rebellion and unwillingness because of sin. How can I turn from them? What does God want me to do?

When Jesus was on earth He often used illustrations of His day; such as the sower going out to sow, or the man journeying, or the Good Samaritan. He used illustrations that people knew about. I am going to use a modern illustration well known in the holiday realm as a package deal. Now a package deal is when people pay a sum of money so that their bus, their flight and their hotel is taken care of. From the moment they leave their house to the moment they come back everything is taken care of in a package deal. Perhaps there is somebody here who would like to be a Christian, and who thinks being a Christian is to somehow enjoy peace. Christianity is not just having a peace or a feeling inside. Salvation is the greatest package deal ever because it was devised of in the eternal counsels. For a man to be saved by Christ at least five things have to happen at the same time. Let me tell you what they are.

First of all you need pardon for every past sin that you committed - that is in salvation's package. Secondly, you need the controlling power of sin cut into by God so that it is no longer all powerful as it was in the past. Thirdly, you need a new nature implanted right inside you by Almighty God. Fourthly, you need the Holy Spirit to indwell you to make that Christian life grow, and fifthly, you need assurance of heaven at death. That is a package deal! Now you might want peace, you might want forgiveness, you might want to make sure you will be all right at the end, but these are only parts. We need the whole package, and my Bible says that those who walk with their God have been given the entire package. Pardon for every past sin, the cutting away of the original controlling power of sin at its source, the new nature implanted when God gives a new heart, the Holy Spirit coming into you and assurance that no matter what happens God will be there to meet you at the end. Now, that is salvation. It is too big just to have one bit - you have to have the lot.

But you have to see what it cost. You need, by the grace of the Holy Spirit of God, to look at the Cross and there see God, the Holy One, pouring your sin, and the sin source itself, into the spotless body of Jesus who had no sin of His own. God was punishing Him instead of you, and you have to go to Jesus, cap in hand, begging and asking Him to be your Saviour, and trust what He did on the Cross as payment for the greatest package deal of all. When you do that you get the whole lot. Some people cry, some people laugh, some people are filled with peace, some people dance, some people are quiet. There are totally different receptions to trusting in what He did on the Cross two thousand years ago. It is not your faith that saves you, it is not your love that saves you, it is not your prayers that save you, it is not your sincerity that saves you - it is Jesus dying on the Cross. My friends, when Jesus gives you the gift of eternal life that He paid for, everything is in it.

But there is something that those who walk with God must be clear about. You now come into fellowship with God. When you fail Him you come back to Him by the way of the Cross, by the way of the broken body and the shed blood of Jesus and you say again, 'Nothing in my hands I bring, simply to the Cross I cling.' Now if you are a sinner here tonight and you want to be saved, it is at the Cross that you find peace. May God help you to turn there.

Can I get five more minutes, for I want to speak just for a moment to the righteous who have turned away, for my message is also to God's people? Among them there are those who walk closely with God, those who profess to walk with Him, and those who do not walk with Him and are in the same condition as those in the Laodicean church - rich and increased with goods, having need of nothing. These are victims of what I call better class blindness - better class, rich and increased with goods, needing nothing, who are deceptively full, who think they need nothing and who have prematurely retired from the work of Christ long before the time due.

Now then, let us look at this just for a moment. Let me say to those who will reject the Son of God that the Bible has warned you of death, and when the Bible speaks of death it means eternal death, an eternal living experience of soul. In the Bible, Hell itself is the penitentiary of the spiritually depraved, the penal settlement of lost souls who, when they heard the gospel, chose to continue to rebel against their Creator. Alas also for those who never heard it and rebel against God. It is a penitentiary for the sin-diseased, the depraved and the Christless. It is a penal settlement where punishment from Almighty God is inflicted upon those who sin against the Creator. The Bible says: 'Hear the word at My mouth and warn them from Me to get to Christ before their death.'

Now to those who are righteous, but are increased with goods. Many who profess the Name of Jesus can remember better days, and I want to speak to such. Your love for Jesus has ebbed - not your knowledge, you still know the Way of the Cross, in fact you are still trusting in the Way of the Cross - but your contact with God and with Christ and with the Holy Spirit is almost non-existent. Your love for Jesus as the Saviour, your love for God who planned your salvation and your love for the Holy Spirit who tolerates your dirt is gone! You have it in the head but not in the heart. I want to speak to those whose love has ebbed, whatever denomination they belong to down here; those whose standards have slipped; those whose standards are not the same as they were in the first six months of their conversion; those who can slip into situations that they would never have tolerated in their first years; those who slip into the situation where they don't worry too much about reading their Bibles, they don't worry too much about prayer, they don't worry too much about attendance in the house of God - those whose standards have slipped, and, even worse, have gone to where they would never have gone when they were walking with God. You may be here tonight whose love has ebbed, whose standards have slipped, whose energy for spiritual things has diminished, whose vision of the things of God is now clouded, whose joy is now ceased, whose walk is now diverted, whose profession is now tarnished, whose life is now empty and whose evangelism in serving God with the bringing of the evangel to others is non-existent.

Am I speaking to such tonight? You who have turned from your righteousness, turned from what you once were. Hear what God says and heed His warning. The complacent, the professional evangelical, the orthodox fiend - tell them that if their love has ebbed, their standard slipped, their energy diminished, their vision of Christ clouded, their joy ceased, their profession tarnished, their life empty, their evangelical effort non-existent, the cause is that they have turned from their righteousness, from the former pattern of personal godliness, from the former path of personal service and commitment, and that the dangers of Laodicea lie upon them.

But I would not stop there. Jesus says at the end: 'I stand at the door and knock.' Just like Ezekiel, He stands at the door with a warning. The warning contains the promise of pardon and restored fellowship but we must respond to the warning and get back to the task. 'But how?' they say, 'It is a long time since I felt anything real in my soul.' Jesus stands as the One who has come by the hill of Calvary, crucified and risen, with pardon and with power and He wants you back. He comes as the One who has been punished for His people's sins, who is able to save us from our particular sins. He stands at the door and knocks by His servants, by conscience, by the Holy Spirit, by the service tonight. But here is the warning. If you are of those who have turned away from your righteousness, you are in danger of becoming God's vomit - you are neither hot nor cold - no good to anyone. So here is the message to those who are without Christ - danger; to those with Christ but who have turned away - danger and death prowls.

Finally, as John pictures Christ Himself standing knocking, will you open the door and let Him in? God help us to do so.

1983

Mr H C MacMillan,
Chief Constable

Lesson for Christian Living
(2 Chronicles 20)

It is good to be here and I thank my colleagues for the privilege of sharing in what is a special Anniversary for the Christian Police Association. From simple and humble beginnings, yet as a result of deep faith and trust in God, the Association has gone from strength to strength in the past 100 years and has been a lifeline and an anchor to generations of police officers. I have had a personal association with the Christian Police Association for 28 years and I look back with gratitude for the help, the friendship and the fellowship I have enjoyed over the years and I cannot let this moment pass without making one further personal comment. I see in the Hall this evening a man I met at my first CPA Annual Meeting in Glasgow 28 years ago. He was at that time nearing retirement but was attending as he had done many times before as one of the Metropolitan Police representatives. I refer to Mr Alex Catto. I cannot remember attending any Annual Meeting since, either in Glasgow or Strathclyde, when Alex was not there like an anchor encouraging and counselling the younger and more inexperienced of his colleagues. It is good to see you here Alex, along with Mrs Catto.

The past 100 years has seen many changes in our social and economic conditions. The majority of people in our country are better fed, better housed, better clothed and, by and large, lead less harsh lives than they did in the past. The police service during the same period has also changed. It has surged forward and policing has become very sophisticated. The span of the century has seen the introduction of new sciences, new technological developments, especially in computers and even new management techniques. There is, however, one thing the past 100 years has not seen - it has not seen a change in human nature or the willingness of man to live in peace and goodwill with his neighbour by obeying God's commands not to kill, steal, covet or bear false witness. Ivan Seifert (an ex RUC officer who gave his testimony at this Anniversary meeting) bears living testimony of man's inhumanity to man and I was thrilled to hear him speak. It is tragic to reflect that last year twelve police officers and reservists were murdered in Ulster and a total of 97 people died as a result of man's hatred, greed and total disregard for the sanctity of human life. These figures represent a drop from the previous year. Again in 1982, 2338 attacks were made on police officers in Ulster - horrific isn't it? Of these, 487 were by petrol bomb attacks, 56 were by explosive devices and 78 were shot at. It makes one sad to contemplate man's inhumanity to man. The riots in our large cities in the past couple of years, the upsurge in crime, particularly serious crime, the warring ideologies, permissiveness, and sexual libertinism, all add strength to the fact that we are becoming degenerate as a nation. Perhaps some of you saw the Panorama programme last Monday night on television when the subject was Venereal Disease. If you did, I'm sure you were as upset as I was at the evidence of depravity and degenerate living portrayed there. What are we who are Christians and who claim to have an alternative lifestyle in Jesus Christ doing about it? Are we living the lives ourselves that we should live in Christ? Are we listening for the promptings of God, are we prepared to act for God, are we prepared to put ourselves out for God? One writer expressed his view in the comment that a Christian cannot jump aboard the lifeboat of salvation and then sit back and say, 'Thank you Lord, Amen.' No! He has got to start looking out of the boat for other survivors. He must attempt to bring other people into the boat of salvation.

In 1965, and not long before he died, the great Swiss theologian Karl Barth was asked what he thought of the religious situation in Britain and on the Continent, and he said, 'What we are seeing is flat-tyre Christianity, the pneuma (which as you may know is the Greek for both spirit and air) has gone out of it' and everybody knows what happens to a pneumatic tyre when it loses its pneuma. Is the church a spiritless, airless carcase? Certainly the church has made little, if any, impact in Britain or the Western world in recent years but the world has made considerable impact on the church. Many professions of Christianity in these days are empty professions and it would be foolish to deny this. Even among those who are truly the children of God by faith in Jesus Christ there is a need for a deeper knowledge of God and a closer relationship with God. Without exception we all need this and until we attain this closer relationship with God, our efforts will produce little fruit. We are told in Daniel 11 verse 32 that the people that know their God shall be strong and do exploits. If we as Christians are to make any stand or have any impact on society we need to be more diligent and humble in our prayers, and more constant in our reading and meditation on the Word of God. We have to come to the means of grace better prepared, more regularly and with more humility. If we do, God, in His mercy and grace, will use these methods to bring us to a deeper knowledge of Himself and a closer intimacy with Him through Jesus Christ.

I am sure there are many here tonight who would say 'Amen' when I say that the Christian life is a life of unparalleled blessing. It is a life of honoured responsibility and of fierce conflict. It is a life which brings great joy but it is a life of battle, and it brings difficulty and disappointment, almost to the point of disillusionment for some. Yet to those who trust and are faithful it is a life which in the end brings unsurpassing victory, and I think Ivan's testimony has expressed this cogently yet simply.

Without doubt the enemy arrayed against the Christian believer is powerful, subtle and well prepared. Yet in the conflict of life the Christian believer is the supreme victor through Jesus Christ, who has met all our foes and overcome them. Paul rejoiced in this and he wrote in his second epistle to the Corinthians, 'Thanks be to God which giveth us the victory through our Lord Jesus Christ.'

I know I am only one of many, but when I want to praise God in my private meditations for His wonderful goodness, and cannot find adequate words of expression, I turn to the Psalms. Similarly, at times when I feel a bit down, disappointed, despondent, and down-hearted as things don't seem to be going right for me, I again turn to the Psalms and read some of the cries of the psalmist. One can almost turn them up at random - Psalm 146: 'Praise the Lord O my soul, I will praise the Lord as long as I live; I will sing praises to my God while I have being.' The next psalm: 'Praise the Lord, for it is good to sing praises to the Lord, for He is gracious and a song of praise is seemly.' Tremendous words, words of great size, but let us not be under any illusion. Although the psalmists were able to write in that way, it did not mean they themselves did not suffer difficulties, setbacks, and real problems in their lives. Of course they did! That's the beauty and the wonder of the Psalms. It is out of such crises or in the midst of them that we share the cries of despair, of doubt and uncertainty of the psalmists and yet we share too the great triumphant notes of praise and thanksgiving to God. Certainly as we come towards the end of the Book of Psalms the flame of praise is shooting up bright and clear, drawing all our attention to God. The Psalms end with: 'Praise, praise, praise to Almighty God; the kings of the earth, the great men, the old men, the young men, praise the Lord. All that hath breath, praise the Lord.' Yes, the believing Christian has the ultimate victory providing he is prepared to place his dependnece upon God, be ready to respond to Him, look to Him in trust and be ready to praise Him and feel the need to praise Him. That is the theme of my message to you this evening. Despite the wickedness and the evil that surrounds us in society, and no one knows that better than a police officer, despite all the disappointments and the disillusionments we encounter in our daily work and in our daily lives, praise brings victory - it brings victory to our living.

The verses we read earlier, in 2nd Chronicles 20, certainly contain a message of encouragement for us. This was a situation where God's people were being threatened by the countries round about them, by the Moabites and the Ammonites, and the people were afraid by reason of the great army that faced them. It was at this point that Jahaziel comes to the king with the words of encouragement and help. 'Don't be afraid by reason of this great multitude,' he says, 'here is what the Lord is saying.' Notice with me quickly four things about this incident and the attitude of the Israelites which I believe are a lesson to us in our Christian living.

First of all, please note *The Principle They Accepted* - verse 15. 'Be not afraid,' says Jahaziel . Why? 'Because the battle is not yours, it is God's.' We are reminded that God is in control. What a tremendous truth that is. The principle they accepted that day was of dependence upon God. The Lord says that without Him, we can do nothing. Is He saying that to someone here tonight? Without Me you can do nothing; the battle that is ahead is not yours, it is Mine; I am in control of the situation. Sometimes we become discouraged in our Christian living and we reach the point where we say, 'Lord, I've done everything I can, I just cannot do any more.' Friends, that is a good point to reach. When we exhaust our own strength we can then hand over to God and give Him control. If anyone here has reached that point, now is the time to hand over and give God complete control. You will find a tremendous difference in every area of your life. The principle the Israelites accepted here was one that we could do well to recall again and again, and it is the principle of dependence upon God. The battle is not yours, it is His.

Look secondly at *The Position They Adopted* - verse 17. If the principle was one of dependence the position was one of readiness. This is a very interesting point. Because they were going to rely on God did not mean that they were to stay in bed, or lie in their tents that day. Not at all! They were dressed and ready for battle - they were ready for action. They were ready to do as directed. The instruction they were given was that they were to set themselves at the ready, to take up their positions for attack and then, having done that, to look away to God and see the victory of the Lord on their behalf. The message is: 'Don't just laze around and feel that you are protected and have to do nothing or you don't feel you should have to do anything.' No! Be ready for whatever the Lord asks you to do in any situation. The Israelites were to look to God. There is a lesson here for all of us. They were not to look to themselves; if they had, they would probably have run away scared stiff, but they were to look to the Lord for victory. It is so very true that if we do look to ourselves and see our own inadequacies, our own failures, our own weaknesses, we do become despondent - or maybe the opposite is true! Perhaps if we look to ourselves, we may be quite pleased with what we see. We see our own abilities, our own ideas, our own ingenuity, and we become quite proud of ourselves, but when we look to God, what a difference! I want you to notice what happened as soon as they did that. Verse 18 says, 'And Jehoshaphat bowed his head with his face to the ground: and all Judah and the inhabitants of Jerusalem fell down before the Lord, worshipping the Lord.'

Here's the third thing - *The Praise They Ascribed To God*. Verses 18 and 21 lay that out for us. They poured out their hearts in thanksgiving to God. We talk sometimes about the prayer of faith but this really was the praise of faith because here they were singing and thanking God for His mercy and His goodness to them before the battle. So often when something happens and we see the results of God's grace and goodness we do give praise to Him. But I wonder how many of us would have had the faith and the trust to praise God in that way before we knew the result or even before the incident took place. That is a very different thing; it is a real challenge to faith and trust. Here we see these people praising God before the battle, taking Him at His word, depending on it, ready and believing that He would do it - the prayer of praise. I wonder if that's true of your praying; it's certainly not always true of *me* to praise the Lord in advance. So often our prayers are a kind of complaining protest to God who seems to manage things so badly for us, full of grievance and self-pity; but here is this great song of praise, 'Give thanks to the Lord for His steadfast love endures for ever.' There they were facing an army that vastly outnumbered them, yet praising the Lord. What a great thing it is to find the secret of praise to God, and what a great thing it is to want to praise God! That is the great message of the men who wrote the Psalms, because they stand at every turn of the road of life, at every corner of experience, and they say, 'Praise the Lord.' When the pressure is on, praise the Lord; when they are up against it, praise the Lord; when they are in the darkest valley, praise the Lord; and that is faith's victory. Praise brings that victory.

71

Some of you may know the story of old Allan Cameron, that great Covenanter, who was lying in the Tolbooth in Edinburgh, imprisoned there for his loyalty to His Saviour and to the Covenant. Suddenly one day, his cell door burst open and some soldiers came in carrying something, and they said to him, 'Look! Look what *we've* got.' Allan Cameron looked, and they uncovered the tray, and it was the head of his son Richard, slain for Christ and for the Covenant. They taunted the old man and he looked in horror at the gruesome sight and staggered back, and then he stopped. He looked and he said, 'It is the Lord, good is the will of the Lord.' That is faith's victory, that is praise in the most awful moment and that was true of the Israelites in this story - ascribing praise to God.

I want you to notice what happened then: *The Power They Appropriated (22-29).* (The same power that old Allan Cameron knew, the same power that Ivan knew, the same power that Job knew when he said, 'The Lord gave and the Lord hath taken away but blessed be the Name of the Lord.') Here we have the expression of the power of victory in the most frightening circumstances.

I remember hearing a soloist singing that lovely song of testimony, *One Step At A Time,* at the Luis Palau Crusade two years ago. On the very night, at the very moment she was singing to an audience of 10,000 people, her young teenage son was dying of a brain tumour in a nearby hospital. This is faith's victory - to be able to praise God in the most bleak and awful circumstances of life. Here it was so for the Israelites. When they began to sing and praise, the Lord set an ambush. When they began to sing and praise, the victory came. I pray that this night of fellowship and praise may just have brought something of the joy of the Lord into our hearts, that it may have encouraged our faith and because of that enable us to praise the Lord for the victory that is ahead. No matter the situations we may have to face in the coming days, may we be able to go forward, trusting God, depending upon Him, having committed ourselves to Him, knowing that the battle is not ours but God's and ready always to take our stand and look to the Lord. But can I interject a word of caution! We can only really praise when our lives are in His hands. It was because the Israelites knew this truth that they were able to begin to feel the confidence that the song brought from their lips. Perhaps for some of us here tonight, before we can sing that song of praise we need to sing the song of commitment and dedication to the Lord. It is only then that we can go forward in confidence to face whatever lies before us, knowing that in God, through Jesus Christ, we have the victory. Our victory will always be traced back to the love of Christ, particularly to that supreme manifestation of it towards us by His death on the Cross.

Finally may I conclude this address by quoting the words of Horatius Bonar who knew the truth of what I have been saying from personal experience. *I know I shall be more than victor through Him who won the fight for me.* May it be so for each of us here tonight. Amen!

1984

Mr Winston Leask
(formerly Faith Mission)

Why I Must Believe in Jesus Christ
(Matthew 16 v 15)

I want to ask you a question. There are many questions which face us in these momentous days in which we live, but I want to ask a question that is more important than any other question we will ever hear. The question is found in Matthew 16:15. Jesus asks His disciples, 'Whom say ye that I am?' What do *you* think of Christ? What does Jesus Christ, the Son of God, mean to you, my friend? Some time ago I heard of a preacher who decided to preach on his doubts. He would have done better to have stayed at home because the Scriptures say that we are to be ready always to give an answer to every man that asketh us a reason of the hope that we have (1 Peter 3:15). I want to leave with you some reasons why we must believe in the Lord Jesus Christ as the living Son of the living God, the only Saviour of mankind.

I want to say I must believe in the Lord Jesus Christ because *no one lived as Jesus lived*. Jesus, the eternal Son of God, lived in a way that no one has ever lived or will ever live.

He was born of a Virgin. In the frail body of that handmaiden of the Lord the eternal Spirit of God produced the human nature of our Lord Jesus Christ, a unique birth; no one was ever born like that before or since.

He lived a life of abject poverty, the Son of God, the Prince of Glory, the One who was ever equal with His Father in Glory! When He was born into this world there was no palace for Him, there were no royal gynaecologists. He was born in a borrowed byre - in a cowshed. He was cradled in a manger that held the food for the beasts. He grew up in obscurity and He lived in poverty. He could say, 'The foxes have holes, the birds of the air have nests but the Son of Man hath not where to lay His head' (Luke 9:58). The Scriptures tell us that by Him all things consist (Colossians 1:17) and without Him was not anything made that was made (John 1:3). He made all things; He owned all things; all the wealth of the worlds flung out into space were His. He created them by the word of His power and yet He had not where to lay His head. He had no pulpit - He had to borrow a boat from which to preach. He had no penny to illustrate the truth that He preached - He had to borrow a penny. When they came to crucify Him, it was upon another man's cross which He carried up Golgotha's hill. When He was buried He was placed in a borrowed tomb.

No one lived as Jesus lived - a voluntary humility. He laid aside the glory that He had in eternity past. You and I cannot understand that. We will never understand it whilst we remain mortal, but when it begins to unfold to us in eternity we will worship the Lamb for ever and ever, and cry, 'Worthy, Worthy, Worthy!' (Revelation 5:11-12). The Lord Jesus Christ, the eternal Son of the eternal Father, with the eternal Spirit of God, in eternity had unspeakable Glory. In His High Priestly Prayer, recorded for us in John 17, He spoke to His Father of the glory which He had with Him before the worlds began. He was equal with His Father, He was the object of heaven's worship. The angels of God who veiled their faces in humility before Him worshipped Him, and waited for the slightest whisper of His command and would speed to do His bidding. The Scriptures tell us that He thought it not a thing to be grasped at to be equal with God but He humbled Himself and being found in fashion as a man, He became obedient unto death, even the death of the Cross. (Philippians 2:6-8). A voluntary humility.

Jesus lived as no other man has ever lived. He was perfectly sinless. I am glad that we preach a Saviour who was sinless. In Him there was no sin. He was spotless; He was pure; He was holy. 'I find no fault in Him,' said Pontius Pilate three times (John 18 and 19). The sinless, spotless Son of God is the only Man, the only Person who has ever lived without sin, the only One who could stand before the multitude and say, 'Which of you convinceth Me of sin?' (John 8 :46). Yes, a sinless, spotless, unique Man. I am glad that we have a Saviour who is incomparable, and those who know and love Him find that He is altogether lovely. There was a time for some of us when He was as a root out of a dry ground. He hath no form nor comeliness (Isaiah 53:2), but those of us who have been saved from our sins, who have been forgiven our past, who have been taken from the gutter and dunghill of sin, have been set among princes. Our names are written in heaven, and we are rejoicing because we are going there, not because we ever deserved to but we are saved by grace through faith (Ephesians 2:8). We think of our Saviour, we sing of our Saviour, we preach of our Saviour and we say that He is the Lily of the

Valley, He's the bright and morning Star, He's the fairest of ten thousand to our souls. He is the altogether lovely One. He is the object of heaven's worship. Those of us who know Him love Him, by His grace.

Do you love the Lord? Are you rejoicing tonight in His love? I am not asking you if you have got religion. I am not asking if your name is on a church roll. I'm not asking what you think of a particular denomination? I'm not asking what do you think of the preacher? - that doesn't really matter! I'm asking you: 'What do you think of my lovely Saviour? What do you think of Jesus? What does He mean to you?' You must believe on the Lord Jesus Christ because nobody lived as Jesus lived.

Secondly, I must believe on the Lord Jesus Christ because *no one died as Jesus died*. Oh yes, others have been crucified. The Romans crucified hundreds of thousands of people but the Scriptures tell us that His visage was so marred more than any man (Isaiah 52:14). The terrible events on Calvary - His suffering not only at the hands of vile sinners but at the hand of an angry God - resulted in His features being distorted beyond recognition. I tell you, nobody died as Jesus died.

Thousands of years before, it was prophesied exactly how He would die. For example, the circumstances were outlined in Isaiah 53, hundreds of years before. It could have been written the day He died on the Cross on Golgotha. Down through the centuries, the prophets of God foretold the death of Christ. We have not time to go into that, but His death was a prophetic death, foretold exactly by men of God moved by the Spirit of God. In fact, it was planned before time began, because He is the Lamb of God that was slain before the foundation of the world. His was a unique death, nobody died as Jesus died.

When He was on the Cross, He dismissed His own spirit and gave up the ghost (John 19:30). Nobody else dies like that. Jesus said, 'I have power to lay down (my life) and I have power to take it again. This commandment have I received of My Father' (John 10:18). No one else dies like that. Your death and my death is in the providence of God. The breath in our bodies at this moment is ours, the next is in the hand of God to give or to withhold, but Jesus could dismiss His own spirit. No one died as Jesus died. His was a unique death.

He died because of sin, not His own sin, but He died because of the sins of others- your sin and mine. Hallelujah! What a Saviour! Each one of us was born spiritually dead because of sin, and each one of us will die physically because of sin; but Jesus died not because of His sin for He had none. On the Cross of Calvary, God made Him to be sin for us who knew no sin; that we might be made the righteousness of God in Him (2 Corinthians 5:21). This is what the Scriptures teach. His was a unique death; nobody died as Jesus died. He died because of the sins of others. What a unique death that was.

The Bible tells us that Jesus tasted death for every man (Hebrews 2: 9). I'm glad that, although I don't know all in this meeting, your background, your problem, the need of your heart, I do know this, that the One who does know has made total provision for the need of the heart of every man and woman, every boy and girl in this meeting. Everyone! How do the Scriptures put it? If any man sin we have an Advocate with the Father, even Jesus Christ, the righteous, and He is the propitiation for our sins and not for ours only but for the sins of the whole world (1 John 2:1-2). Beware of a preacher who belittles the atonement of Christ! Beware of preaching that does not make Christ available to every sinner because the Word of God tells us that He tasted death for every man. I must believe in the Lord Jesus Christ because no one died as Jesus died.

Friend, my dear friend, Jesus died for you. Jesus, in His spotless, sinless body, took your sin and mine all the way to Calvary, nailing it there.

Bearing shame and scoffing rude,
In my place condemned He stood,
Sealed my pardon with His Blood,
Hallelujah! What a Saviour!

Is He your Saviour? What think ye of Christ?

Thirdly, I must believe in the Lord Jesus Christ as the Son of God because *no one rose from the dead as Jesus did.* His resurrection makes Christianity unique. If you travel this world visiting the great religious centres, you will find the tombs of the great religious leaders and you will be shown the place where their bones lie rotting and decaying, but, could you find the grave of the Lord Jesus Christ there would be no rotting bones, because He is alive and He lives in the power of an endless life (Hebrews 7:16).

Others have been raised from the dead, but not as Jesus arose. There are recorded instances in the Word of God of people having risen from the dead but theirs was a different resurrection to that of Jesus, because all who have risen from the dead have had to be raised from the dead. Jesus was not only raised from the dead but He arose! His was the power over death, hell and the grave - they could not hold Him. Truly His was a unique resurrection. Had Jesus not risen from the dead there would have been no other resurrections. He became the first fruits of them that sleep (1 Corinthians 15:20).

Those who have been brought back to physical life have all since died. They await the certain final resurrection on the last day, when He, who rose from the dead as no man has ever risen from the dead, shall return with the shout that will wake all the dead. And because He lives we shall live also. When you and I are called to depart this body, be it sooner or later, that is not the end. There is the resurrection of the just, the blood-washed people of God, to eternal life and happiness. The same Scriptures that teach this great truth also teach the resurrection of the Christ-rejecter to eternal damnation. Strong words, but the Word of God! I must believe in the Lord Jesus Christ because no one rose again as Jesus rose.

Finally, I must believe on the Lord Jesus Christ because *no one spake as Jesus spake*. What a subject - the sayings of Christ.

There were those who were sent out to find fault, to try and trap Him. Those messengers had to return to the Sanhedrin, the religious leaders of the day, and say that never man spake like this Man (John 7:46). The multitudes marvelled at the gracious words that proceeded out of His mouth because He taught them as One having authority (Matthew 7:29). Never man spake like this Man.

About children He said, 'Suffer the little children to come unto Me' (Matthew 19: 14). There are some boys and girls in this Rally tonight. I wonder, boys and girls, what does the Lord Jesus mean to you?

Have you opened your heart to Him and received Him as your Lord and Saviour?   You must, and you can tonight. He says, 'Come unto Me.'

The same Saviour who spoke so to children, spoke wonderful words to every human need that ever existed. When He was with the bereaved, what did He say to them? 'I am the Resurrection and the Life' (John 11:25).   Nobody else can say that!   When bereavement comes, this old world has nothing to give you. When that chilling hand invades your home you will only hear the words, 'I am the Resurrection and the Life,' if the Lord Jesus Christ is your Saviour. How did He speak to the dead; to Jairus' daughter, to the widow of Nain's son, to Lazarus who had been buried several days previously? He spoke with a power that woke the dead. When He was confronted with the grave of Lazarus, He lifted up His voice and He cried, 'Lazarus, come forth!' (John 11 :43). Why did He say that?   I believe if Jesus had not said, 'Lazarus,' the whole graveyard would have come forth!   Why? Because nobody spake as Jesus spake. He speaks with unique power and authority.   No one else can call forth the dead to life, save this Lord of life and glory, the eternal Son of God.

How did Jesus speak to sinners?   We should all be interested in what Jesus had to say to sinners because we are all sinners. When a sinner was brought to Jesus, what did He say? 'Thy sins are forgiven,' (Luke 7:48); and no one else can say that but Jesus. No one else can forgive sin. An old lady lay on her deathbed. Amongst those who called to see her was a man, and when he entered her room she said, 'Who are you?' He said, 'I am the priest, I have come to forgive you your sins.' Calling him over, she took his hand, examined it closely, then pushed it away, saying, 'Sir, you are no priest, you are an impostor. The Man who forgives my sins has nail-prints in His hands.'

What about your sin? Has it been forgiven? That will depend on what you think of Jesus. That will depend on what you have done with Jesus. This unique, precious Saviour is here as the only One who can forgive sin and save your precious, never-dying soul. So, without apology, I repeat the questions, 'What think ye of Christ?' and, 'What will you do with Jesus tonight?' Upon your answers to those questions will hang your eternal destiny, my dear friend. The time is coming, if you reject Him, when you will be asking, 'What will He do with me?'

He says, and I quote this in conclusion, 'Come unto Me all ye that labour and are heavy laden and I will give you rest' (Matthew 11:28). Will you come tonight? Will you say 'Yes' to Jesus? Will you come to know and love my Saviour? He is the wonderful Son of God who loved me and gave Himself for me. Will you say, 'I will love Him, I accept Him, I repent of my sin and I take Him as my Lord and my all.' If you will, He will receive you, and you will come to know Him whom to know is Life eternal.

You must believe on the Lord Jesus Christ.

1985

Rev. Dr Robert McGhee,
Church of Scotland, Falkirk

The Woman of Samaria (John 4)

When I came on to this platform tonight I intended to preach from the Book of Habakkuk. Now I am sure that it is much easier to find John chapter 4 than it is to find Habakkuk. However as I listened to the emphasis that has come through in the Delegates Report, in the testimonies and in the singing of the songs of Zion, I felt led to centre on none other than our Lord and Saviour Jesus Christ.

I ask you to take some time within the next few days to read Habakkuk for yourself; there are only three chapters, but read Habakkuk along with your daily newspaper and see how up to date the Word of God is. Here was a man who was crying to God, 'Oh God, how long, how long?' as many a Christian is crying today, but who came through to the point where he was saying, 'In wrath, remember mercy, revive Thy work in the midst of the years.' May you take time to read it and may God by His Spirit speak to you. But now I want to share with you from John chapter 4.

When I read this chapter it takes me back to the days of 1955 in the Kelvin Hall in Glasgow when Dr Billy Graham was here for the All Scotland Crusade. These were indeed blessed days. My home town is Port Glasgow on the Clyde and I can remember during the six week campaign in the Kelvin Hall that from my home church, three nights every week, a bus filled with people of all ages would go to hear him. When the rallies were held in Ibrox or Hampden we had a special train from the town, and I can thank God here tonight that I had one sister converted at Ibrox and one sister converted at Hampden. This chapter brings back to me the message that Billy Graham preached one evening when there was such a company in the Kelvin Hall that many were asked to leave and go into an overflow. I was numbered with that overflow, hearing him preach from John chapter 4, and I never come to this chapter but that I hear the voice of Dr Billy Graham speaking through it. But I pray above all tonight that we will meet with and hear the voice of the Lord Jesus Christ.

Here we find Jesus, and we are told that He left Judaea and departed again into Galilee and He must needs go through Samaria. He *must needs* go through Samaria. There were three roads that Jesus could have taken. He could have taken the coast road orHe could have taken the road through Perea, as well as the other road through Samaria itself. Perhaps it seemed not very significant what road would be taken, for after all they were making their way back to the north from Judaea to Galilee; but surely God the Father had a purpose in directing His Son to go this particular road, for it was on that road that he was to meet a woman, a woman who was to be changed and through her testimony was to reach many others so that, though Jesus came to that town simply regarded as a Jew, when He left that town of Sychar they looked upon Him as the Saviour of the world.

He must needs go through Samaria. I wonder tonight, as we are sitting here, how many of us have gone through certain experiences in life that we would never have chosen to go through. I know that I can testify to that. I can remember just a few years ago sitting in a situation with the tears running down my cheeks and knowing the truth of the words of the psalmist, 'My tears have been my meat, day and night', and saying to a friend there are roads that we have to walk that we would never have chosen to walk but when we are on them we have to walk them. He must needs go through Samaria! You have heard the testimony of our brother (Victor Buchanan from Ulster who attended this Anniversary meeting and gave his testimony) here tonight, who has had to walk roads that he would never have chosen to walk, but you see the 'must needs'. God can take them, overrule them, and bring His purposes to pass. I wonder how many of us have come into a relationship with the Lord Jesus Christ because there was a particular circumstance or experience or problem in life. It was dark in those days, the road was rough and steep and we longed for a way out, but when we look back along the road of life, we can see that God was there and at work because He wanted us, like this woman, to meet His Son who would give us the water of life. He must needs go through Samaria.

I wonder why you are here tonight? Is there someone here who does not really want to be here, but you did not want to disappoint a friend and so you came? But you are here also because God meant you to be here. Perhaps God has been speaking to you right from the beginning of this gathering, and you are aware of it. Don't shut out His voice but, like this woman, open your heart and come to Jesus.

Jesus remained at Jacob's well when the disciples went to the town to buy food. He was wearied with the journey and sat by the well. Are we not blessed with a Saviour who knows and cares and understands? We have a Saviour who feels with that family in Ulster tonight whose two sons have been taken so tragically and suddenly. Do we not have a Saviour who enters into that home, a Saviour who wept His tears by Lazarus' tomb? Does Jesus not weep His tears tonight? Do we not have One in heaven who feels for us in all our infirmities, who understands us in all our weaknesses? This is the blessing of knowing Jesus Christ. It is not knowing someone who is divorced from the reality of life as we find it, but we come to a Saviour who knows what it means to be weary, to be tired, to be hungry, to be discouraged, to be disappointed. Yes! He knew it all in life, and here He was wearied with the journey, and while the others went to the city He sat there waiting on them coming back.

But into the picture that day there came a woman. Oh, we might say that she should never have been out at that time as noon was not the time to come to draw water. Surely she should have come later in the day when the other women would come. Why did she come at that time? Oh! Jesus knew, and as the story unfolds so we realise why she came at that time; it was because she could not face the other women. They knew about her life. There was no way she was going to be there to hear them talking about her and so she came at noon. I am sure, as she saw the man sitting there, her only intention was to come and draw the water and get back into the city again. But what a man she was going to meet, for as she came to the well it was Jesus who said, 'Give Me to drink'. She was very taken aback; after all she was a Samaritan and He was a Jew. He was a true blue, but the blood that ran

86

through the Samaritan's veins was mixed so the Jews had no dealings with the Samaritans. In addition, He was a man, and a man sometimes would not even speak to his own wife outside. Yet Jesus said, 'Give Me a drink.'

The conversation began. She said, 'You are a Jew and you are asking drink of me, a woman of Samaria?' He replied, 'If thou knewest the gift of God and who it is that sayeth unto thee, "Give Me to drink," you would have asked of Him and He would have given you living water.' Perhaps she was becoming mesmirised and getting a little lost. She said, 'But sir, you've nothing to draw with, the well is deep. How can you get living water, running water, and share it with me when you are the one who is asking me to give you a drink because I am the one who has brought the bucket with me?' Then she showed she had a little religious knowledge. She said, 'Are you greater than our father Jacob who gave us this well?' Then Jesus said, 'Whosoever drinketh of this water shall thirst again but whosoever drinketh of the water that I shall give him shall never thirst, but the water that I shall give him shall be in him a well of water, springing up into everlasting life.' Then she said unto Him, 'Sir, give me this water, that I thirst not, neither come hither to draw.' Oh yes! the conversation had taken another turning.

Perhaps you have come here tonight intending to go home the same way as you came, but Jesus Christ is speaking to you just as real tonight as He spoke to that woman so long ago, and He is offering you that living water.

What did the woman say? 'Sir, give me this water that I neither thirst, neither come hither to draw.' But then Jesus had something to say to her: ' Go, call your husband.' At that the woman looked into the eyes of Jesus and we are told that she replied that she had no husband. He said to her, 'Yes, there is truth in what you are saying because you have had five husbands and the man that you are now living with is not your husband.' She said, 'Sir, I perceive that you are a prophet.'

We have seen the humanity of Jesus in His tiredness, in His thirst, but surely here we see the divinity of Jesus. Here was One who could look into that woman's life and know all its details. He had not met her before, and no one had come and given Him the story of her life. Did she not go and tell the men at the gate of Sychar, 'Come see a man that told me all things that ever I did.' She was taken aback, but that is the way it is with Jesus and with each of us here tonight. He knows everything about us. He knows the circumstances of life, He knows our home situation, our family situation, our work situation, our unemployment situation. Yes and He knows the skeletons in the cupboard! He opened the door in that woman's life when He said that she had had five husbands and the man she was living with was not her husband. Men and women, if Jesus was to take each of us aside separately and begin to tell us about our lives there would be blushes on our cheeks.

She tried to get out of it at that point. She said, 'Our fathers worshipped in this mountain and you say that in Jerusalem is the place where men ought to worship.' She was trying to lead Jesus up a religious road. What Jesus was saying to her was becoming too pointed. It was really getting down into her being where it hurt, and she did not like to have the searching eyes of Christ seeing all this in her life and so she took Him up this side road to speak about religion.

Isn't that the way so many cover-up today? I go to church, I go to the Mission Hall, I live a good life! As a minister of the gospel, often in a time of sorrow, I hear these words being said by some. I am sure that there are many good people but our goodness never saved us. Our righteousness, as the Scripture says, is as filthy rags. No! We need a righteousness beyond our own and if I had preached from Habbakuk tonight, we would have read the word, that word that came to Martin Luther, and that brought about the Reformation which swept through Europe: 'The just shall live by faith'. This righteousness comes to anyone, not by what he or she does or is, but by their trusting in the Lord Jesus Christ and His finished work at Calvary.

Then she said, 'I know that when the Messiah comes, He will tell us all things.' Jesus said, 'I that speak unto thee am He. At first, she looked on Him as a Jew, then she saw in Him a prophet. Now she sees Him as the Messiah. How do you see Jesus tonight? Would you say Jesus is a good man, would you go beyond that and identify Jesus with some of the great prophets of the past or are you willing to go beyond even that and say with Peter, 'You are the Christ, the Son of the living God?'

You who are here tonight, it is your door He is knocking on. 'Behold, I stand at the door and knock. If any man (or woman) hear My voice and open the door I will come in to him and will sup with him and he with Me.' Oh! Come down from that religious road, come down from the road of your own goodness, your own standing, and come and meet Jesus on *His* road, for He is the Way, and no man comes unto the Father but by Him. Hear Him knocking on the door of your heart in these moments. You do not have to wait until this message is finished. Even now, where you sit, where you are, you can be opening the door by saying to Jesus, 'I do believe that You are the Christ, the Son of the living God.'

What was the impact on that woman? She left her water pot, and made her way back into the town and there she went up and with boldness spoke to the men who stood around its gates. There she bore her first testimony, a simple yet powerful testimony, 'Come see a man which told me all things that ever I did: is not this the Christ?'

Our brother, Victor, gave his testimony tonight. Do you have a testimony to give? A testimony that is up to date? Many have a testimony that belongs to the past, and thank God for that, but we should not only be speaking of what Jesus meant to us ten, twenty or thirty years ago, but speaking of what Jesus means to us here and now, and to have the courage to say to others, 'Come see a Man who told me all things that ever I did.' It is not Africa or India or South East Asia or South America that is the missionary situation of the world today. The missionary situation of the world today is in Scotland, and there are many who need Christian people in Scotland to speak of Christ in a humble yet bold way. Bring a friend under the sound of the gospel wherever it is preached, so that they might come to see this Man for themselves, the Man of Calvary.

But what was the outcome? The disciples returned and were taken aback to discover that He had been speaking with the Samaritan woman. But the outcome of the witness of that woman meant that many of the Samaritans of that city believed in Him. Is this not an encouraging word, and a challenging word, to many a Christian? If we are Christ's here tonight, then are we not saved to serve? Does Jesus not give us the commission, 'You shall be witnesses unto Me, in Jerusalem, in Judaea, in Samaria and unto the uttermost parts of the world.' Begin where you are, where you live, where you work, among your friends, to be His witness?

We are told that through this woman's simple witness many came to believe on the Lord Jesus Christ and instead of Jesus just passing through that city they pled with Him that He would stay on for a short time. He stayed there two more days and many more believed because of His own word. They said unto the woman, 'Now we believe, not because of thy saying for we have heard Him ourselves, and know that this is indeed the Christ, the Saviour of the world.' What an impact! And an impact because Jesus must needs go through Samaria, because God had ordained that there His Son would meet with a woman that many had no time for, who had been written off in her class of society; but a woman that came to realise the truth about herself when Jesus spoke about the water of life. She bore witness to Jesus, so that, when Jesus left two days later, many in that city had come to believe that He was the Saviour of the world. That is what He is tonight; He is the Saviour of the world. But is He your personal Saviour? Can you say, 'Now I believe, not because of what you are saying but I have heard Him for myself and know that this is indeed the Christ, the Saviour of the world?'

I am sure that this would be the greatest blessing of this gathering here that the angels in heaven were even now recording a name or more than one name in the Lamb's Book of Life. Here at this fifth Anniversary meeting of the CPA in Inverness, you met Jesus and Jesus met you. I pray God that you will open your heart and say, as the children sing in their chorus:

'Into my heart, into my heart,
Come into my heart, Lord Jesus;
Come in today, come in to stay,
Come into my heart, Lord Jesus.'

1986

Rev Robert MacLeod,
Free Church of Scotland, Tarbert

The Rich Fool (Luke 12 v 16-21)

It is a pleasure to be here with you all on this your Annual Rally.   Let us look at God's Word together and may we know His blessing. We will read in Luke 12, perhaps in particular at verses 16 to the end, and taking for our text verse 20, where God said to a man, *'You fool, this night your soul will be required of you; then whose will those things be which you have provided?'*

Now, I am sure that many people here this evening who are Christians, including many police officers, would vouch to the fact that, on many occasions, as a Christian, one has been viewed a fool. Perhaps you can remember the first shift you went on with ten, fifteen, maybe twenty men and you were the only Christian and you had to bear testimony to the fact. You can remember perhaps the night you spoke to the first colleague, maybe on nightshift, and for the rest of the nightshift it was a long, long time because you sensed his attitude as one of total indifference and one that regarded you as an absolute idiot.

There are many of you who have neighbours from whom you have encountered that same sentiment. Because your values are different, you are fools. Perhaps you are in business, and have many colleagues who are of the same opinion. There may be ministers here this evening who on many occasions, either, in your own congregation or in other congregations, where you have stood up to preach the old, old story of the Cross, have sensed this indifference. You have been told to your face that what you preach is absolute nonsense. The great legacy of Christianity is that in every generation the world has viewed it as foolishness. This evening I want to remind ourselves of something very, very important: it is the Christian who is wise, not the unbeliever.

I am not saying to you that the Christian life is one bed of roses with no problems, no difficulties, no trials, no troubles. I would be telling a lie and I would be denying the reality of the Christian faith if I were to say it was, because all who love Christ will vouch for the fact that though it is marvellous to be a Christian it is also very difficult. The Christian life is a trial, it is a warfare, because there is the enemy at every quarter, at every corner in every day, sometimes very obvious, sometimes very subtle; but the Christian is confronted daily with the reality that he is in the midst of a warfare because he is on the side of the King of Kings, since he has moved camps from that of darkness to that of light, when he turned from following the prince of this world to giving obedience, honour, glory and worship to the God who has no equal and is therefore matchless.

The Christian is the winner, even though confronted with all these difficulties. We are reminded by John that the Christian is an overcomer. This is his experience because of what Christ has done in his heart and life. He is conqueror, winner, and overcomer because of the new dynamic relationship he has with Jesus Christ. He is winner also because of the glorious prospects he has on account of the promise and commitment by Christ to come again to take the believer to where He is to share an endless relationship and experience with Him in glory. When I say that I say it in order to reiterate the fact that the non-Christians are the ones that are the fools. I want us to turn to this parable this evening to find out exactly why such people are fools. I want us to see that it is not my opinion, nor is it the opinion of the church, nor is it the opinion of a minister - it is the opinion of God.

Jesus was interrupted by a man who obviously had been untouched by all the serious matter that Jesus had been speaking of (Chapters 10-12) and he interrupts Him with a very earthly and materialistic kind of question. Jesus uses it to show how foolish of man to lay up his eternal security on the things of this world. Notice first of all that the assessment is not made on account of the fact that a man is successful. This is not why a man is classed a fool, because God nowhere condemns a man for being successful. Throughout the Scriptures there are many men who were not only believers but very wealthy. Even in this parable the implications are that it is God who made him so prosperous in the first place. Why then do we say men are losers who place all their confidence in the abundance of the things they possess? Why are such men deemed foolish by the great God who made them, before whom they must all stand when He will finally separate those who love Him from those who hate Him?

First of all this man is deemed a fool *because he lived with no place in his life for God*. He had no place in his thoughts because his thoughts were taken up solely with himself. His thoughts focused on all that he had and all that he planned to do. This man, in all practical terms, was an atheist. God never came into his reasoning. It did not matter how often his conscience told him he was accountable to God he blanketed from his mind the reality of God. Often he strolled across his fields, surveying all he possessed, looking up into the heavens and reading the skies as to what sort of day it would be tomorrow, looking into the majesty of the heavens as they declare the glory of God. Yet he did not think about God.

Further he lived with no place for God in his thankfulness. He was a very prosperous successful farmer. His barns were so full that they could not hold all that he had accumulated and so he needed bigger barns in order to store more. For one moment has he stopped to give God thanks for the sunshine that brought the seed forth? Does he thank God for his abilities that made him so successful? We find in this parable that no place is given to thanking God.

Notice also that he lived with no time for God. He had time for speculation as to how he might better invest his income; there was time for strategy about how to produce more; how to accumulate more storage place and more grain; how to better distribute it in order to bring in more income. There was time for eating, drinking, and merriment; but there was no time, not one moment, for the living God.

I am asking you, this evening, if this fits your experience? No matter how much your mind tells you God is, you deny it. No matter how much God has given you, because He shines on the unjust and the just with His favour in providence, you have never lifted up your heart to God and said, 'Thank you!' You have never thanked God for the breath you are breathing today. Have you thanked Him for the home you live in, for the family you possess, for the job you hold down, for the income that keeps you secure? Have you ever given time to it? You have time for all your plans, like the farmer. You have times for all your speculation, for dreaming great dreams for the future but how much time have you given to Christ in the last week? How much time have you given to the Saviour, whether you be eighty, seventy or seventeen?

But I want you to notice also that this man was a fool *because he lived a pretend existence*. The pretence existence that he lived is reflected in several ways. He lived first of all denying the fact that he was mortal. It seems that the more he accumulated, the more he pushed back from his mind the fact that he must die and that he must meet his Maker. He forgot he was a spiritual creature, made to glorify God and ultimately to stand before God. He thinks that life is going to go on, and on, and on, and on, and never end. This pretence many of us live. When we are young we think we have all the time in the world. We intend to take seriously these matters in a number of years time. This man lived with this pretence but reality caught up with him so suddenly. Death is as near the back of a young man as it is to the front of an old man.

But that was not the only way his pretence was seen. You notice that he also believes that things will satisfy and bring the answers to all his deep cravings. It is suggestive that no matter how much he accumulated he is still totally dissatisfied and unable to say he has got enough and is content. He lived a pretence existence. Do you live like that? Do you live in a make-believe world that denies the fact that you are a mortal creature that will ultimately face the Valley of the Shadow? Do you live in the make-believe world that imagines that the abundance of things is what really matters? This man lived with that kind of mentality, and God's assessment is this; he was a fool because a man's life does not consist in the abundance of the things he possesses.

But thirdly, he was a fool *because he lived a life that was pitiable*. Looking into the experience of this particular man, I am sure there are many of us who would say that if only we had a portion of his fortune what a great answer it would be to our particular problems this evening. But I want to suggest to you that God says this man's life is pitiable and there is nothing in it to be coveted because it is a life that is foolish. Why is it foolish? It is foolish because he is so contemptuous of everyone else. He is utterly selfish, thinking only of Number One all the time, and that kind of man possesses no endearment, no attraction to God or even man, when man is honest about this kind of individual.

But not only is he pitiable because of his contemptuous attitude to everyone else, he is pitiable because of his captivation with himself - he is your Number One egotist. He is the type of man who will stand at the mirror many a morning and put his shoulders back, and marvel at what he is, marvel at imagined dignity, and all that he has accumulated. How many times does 'I' or 'my' come into the picture throughout this parable? Twelve times in a matter of four or five verses . 'I' and 'my' permeates this man's character. He lived for himself.

Notice also he is pitiable because of his carelessness over his own soul. Throughout this parable as he is captivated by himself and lives with no time for God, this man is careless over the most important thing that a man can deal with - the safety of his soul and his rightness with God before he meets his Maker. I have a picture of this man in our own generation. I have an image of him as the kind of man who comes home from his work in the evening, the fire is lovely and burning hot, the meal is being served, he has talked a little with his wife and perhaps talked a little with his children if he has spared the time. He has eased himself into his big arm-chair, taking a drink, relaxing with a cigarette or a cigar. Around him lies the papers of success, the journals of farm-management, the journals of financial investment, and as this man sits in his easy chair, is there a thought for God, is there a thought over the safety of his soul? No! There is not a thought!

I again picture this man thinking as he eases into the chair, 'Sure, the minister was round last week; he talked a lot about eternal security, about the necessity of faith in the Lord Jesus Christ, about the need for sins forgiven, about the life that he could experience if Jesus came into his life and changed it.' But he pushes himself further back. 'Oh, our minister, he's too zealous, he's a bit fanatical, he's a bit too narrow minded, he's a bit extreme. I'll give him my donation, I'll uphold the cause, I'll be seen at times within the walls of the church, but concerning my soul there is no need to be alarmed . All is well with my soul because my barns are full, my bank balance is good, my bank manager never has to rebuke me for being overdrawn. My family are well fed, they're well thought of.'

'All is well with my soul' is the man's own estimation of his position. Peace, peace, he tells himself. Never mind the fanatical approach, never mind the need for responding to the invitation of the gospel, never mind conversion, never mind the new birth, never mind the significance of the death of Jesus Christ 2000 years ago. He lives and believes a lie and he takes no care for his soul. Are you like that this evening? Is this you in the parable that we read?

But this man also is a fool because *he lived with the wrong perspective.* We so often live as men and women who have just got seventy years if we are fortunate. We forget we are men and women who are made for eternity. We must ultimately meet our Maker, either to be drawn into the glory that He has prepared for His people or to be cast into that place that He Himself calls hell and describes as a place where there is only weeping and wailing and gnashing of teeth. A place where there is only the realisation in peoples' minds that they were foolish when they ignored the days of opportunity, when they were stupid in not responding to the invitation to come, when their hearts told them there was a God and that there is a Judgment Day when they would be separated from Him.

How wrong this man's perspective was! 'I have laid up much, take your ease, I have many years,' is his dream. Is that yours? It certainly was not the apostle Paul's for he said to live was good but to die was gain, because to die was far better. When Paul is defending the great reality of the resurrection to the church in Corinth, he reminds us of the perspective of the believer and the reason why the believer is not a fool but an overcomer, a winner, one that is more than a conqueror. When he writes of the nature of that resurrected body he says, 'In a moment, in the twinkling of an eye, we shall be changed' because we shall rise to live eternally with God. There is eternity, and woe to us if we ignore that reality and that perspective as we live our lives. You go back even into the Old Testament with Abraham many years before Christ came, and before man knew with confidence that the grave was not the end. But yet Abraham looked through the years, through the tunnel that he saw to eternity, and what did he look for? He looked for a city whose Maker was God and whose existence would be eternal. Is that your perspective, or is your perspective that of the fool this evening because you have not reckoned with it and you are not particularly interested in it?

Well, if your perspective is earthly this evening, like this man's, let me conclude by showing how he was so foolish. Yes, he lived, and lived a marvellous life doubtless. He lived with all the accoutrements of good living, and I could doubtless say that he enjoyed it, and there are many things in this man's life that are commendable - he fended for his family, he used his initiatives, he put the gifts God gave him into practice and God blessed him abundantly. However, though he lived with all these seeming plusses, his life was lived so foolishly, and ultimately you notice the climax of his foolishness is seen in that sudden moment, when he died that very night as he speculated on the future and the many more years he had to enjoy his wealth. Notice he lived a fool but notice also that this man died a fool, and you also will die a fool, if you die unprepared to meet your Maker with sins not forgiven, without love for Christ and without any endeavour to glorify the Name of God.

Notice three things in the man's death. Notice how sudden it was - tonight! tonight! Now Roy and Tom (Roy Robinson and Tom Davison who were attending this meeting as visitors from Ulster) , they live with the reality every day they step out of their homes that perhaps in a moment they can be gone. But you do not have to be living under the threat of the bullet for the call of God to come so suddenly. It can come so suddenly even now.

But notice also how solemn it was. When his end comes it is God that he has to reckon with because it is God who says to him that tonight his soul will be required of him.

But notice how sad it was because though he lived with everything that was possible to achieve at his fingertips, where did it leave him as he stands before his Maker? Jesus tells us - bankrupt! With absolutely nothing! He could not call upon his riches nor present his abilities. He could not use all the initiative that he had put into practice as possible reasons for God not to cast him from His presence and to put him to that place where the rich man in the story of Lazarus ended up, lifting up his eyes, being in torments. None of these things could save or help him; none of these things mattered when he stood before his God. And I say to you this evening as we close that if you live without God and should tonight God come and call you and you die without Him, it is not the end. The Scriptures tell us that just as it is appointed unto man once to die there follows the judgment. Now the rich man faced that judgment, and he would face it bankrupt.

Is this the way you would meet Him this evening? Would you stand before Him, unable to tell Him that you loved His Son, unable to tell Him that you knew of His grace and His love, unable to tell Him that you had experienced His forgiveness, unable to tell Him that you knew of that moment when He lifted you up from the miry clay and set your feet upon the Rock. If you are unable to stand before Him with these reasons and stand before Him covered in the blood of Christ, cleansed from sin that separates us from God, then you will stand with this kind of bankruptcy, you will stand a fool.

I wonder if I am speaking to a police constable who has maybe not long joined the force and is looking ahead to many years to enjoy.   Have you considered, as you have thought through the years of police service, of the most important priority of all - the Lord Jesus Christ and your relationship to Him?

I wonder if I am speaking to any officer of rank who has enjoyed perhaps many years of police service, enjoyed the experience of promotion, enjoyed the stability of the job, and you are looking ahead to the prospect of retirement.   Have you, and I ask you with all earnestness, have you made certain of your calling, have you made certain of a right relationship with the Lord Jesus Christ?

I wonder if I am speaking to a visitor this evening. If God came to you this evening would His assessment be of you that you are a fool or that you are wise? If God comes to any of us this evening, where would we spend eternity? Let us not be fools.

The Lord Jesus Christ came into the world to make men that are losers, winners, to make men and women who have no real standing before God, individuals who can stand before Him in complete confidence. He came into the world to deal with the problem of our foolishness, of our lostness, in order that eternity might not be fearful but glorious and be looked forward to with expectation. We can be like Paul who anticipated it with joy because of all that it holds out to the man or woman who has bowed the knee to the Lord Jesus Christ. So may God help you not to be a fool but to come to Christ this evening. Amen!

1987

Rev. Roderick Morrison,
Church of Scotland, Stornoway.

The Father Giving Sinners to Jesus
(John 6 v 37)

Will you turn with me in your Bibles to John 6:37 where it says: *All that the Father giveth Me shall come to Me, and him that cometh to Me, I will in no wise cast out.*

At this particular time in the ministry of Jesus Christ, a great many of the Jewish people had doubts about Him, and they were rejecting His ministry. They were murmuring against Him. They were murmuring for example against His claim that He was the Bread of heaven. In verse 52, we find this written, 'The Jews therefore strove among themselves saying, How can this Man give us His flesh to eat?' In this chapter Jesus teaches many of the great and important doctrines of the Christian faith. In this verse alone, we learn about the Sovereignty of God, Election, Effectual Calling, Redemption and Salvation.

Jesus is making quite clear that no person can be saved unless that person comes to Him. He also teaches that that person cannot come unless he is among those that the Father has given to the Son from all eternity. Then He emphasises the fact of human responsibility in the words, 'him that cometh unto Me, I will in no wise cast out.' So it is clear from this chapter, and from this verse in particular, that the work of redemption will never be frustrated by unbelief, whether it is the unbelief of the Jews, or the unbelief of anyone else. God has His people, and those people will come in every age and in every generation and they shall be gathered from the east, and the west, and the north, and the south. They will be effectually and savingly called into the Kingdom of God in every age.

There are many in the visible church of Jesus Christ who maintain that man in his fallen natural state can exercise his free will and believe in Jesus Christ at any time, and that it is possible for every one of Adam's race to be saved. This teaching produces the attitude of mind, that a person is unwilling to renounce the ways of sin, because he fondly imagines that at some particular moment, as he comes near the shores of eternity, that he will trust in Jesus Christ and that he will be saved. I believe that there is not a more subtle snare of the devil than that teaching. To believe that having wasted your life and your days in forgetfulness of God and in sin and then, by your own efforts, come to trust in Jesus Christ as you enter into eternity, is something that I don't find any support for in the Bible. The doctrine of Human Depravity teaches us that fallen human minds, apart from the grace of God, are opposed to everything that is godly or spiritual. The human mind without the grace of God recoils from God and from everything that God commands. To believe in the Lord Jesus Christ as Saviour is one thing that the natural man will not and cannot do except with the help of the grace of God. Jesus underlines this truth in verse 65: 'No man can come unto Me except it were given unto him of My Father.'

We are going to look at three things that appear

Force for Christ

from this verse. The first thing is *The Gift of the Father* - All that the Father *giveth* Me. We often think of the gift of the Father as the giving of His Only and Well-Beloved Son, Jesus Christ, to be the Saviour of sinners, and the apostle Paul quite rightly says, 'Thanks be to God for His unspeakable gift.' Indeed He is the Unspeakable Gift, the Gift that crowns every other gift that was given or ever will be given in this world. But there is another gift that the Bible speaks about, a mysterious gift, and it is the gift that the Father gave the Son in the counsels of eternity, before time began, when God the Father willed that a remnant of the human race be saved and become His people for ever. A great multitude was chosen in Christ before the foundation of the world and, as Paul says, they were chosen that they should be holy and without blame before Him in love (Ephesians 1:4). They were originally in the Father's hand, chosen by Him and belonging to Him as Creator, but He gave them to the Son as a gift.

God the Father is often portrayed by some people as a stern Being seeking to punish sin while Christ the Son suffers for sin and takes away the wrath of an angry God. Yet the truth is that God the Father was behind every aspect of the work of salvation. He chose those who will believe in Christ as Saviour and He gave them to the Son. Jesus Himself says in John 17:6, 'Thine they were and Thou gavest them Me.' The Father draws them to Christ in every generation, by placing a holy constraint within their hearts. It amazes us at times when we see what kinds of people are converted in our congregations, churches, and parishes. Think of others in Scripture such as Zacchaeus and Saul of Tarsus. They would be the last

107

people you would ever imagine that would be followers of Jesus Christ. But both Zacchaeus and Saul of Tarsus were converted, and down the years the Christian church has been marked by similar surprises. All we can do is stand in awe before God and recognise His sovereignty in the work of salvation. God the Father is drawing unworthy sinners like you and me to Himself by His grace. That is what happens when a soul is converted to Christ.

The verse speaks here of the Father giving in the present tense-all that the Father *giveth*. There is a certain sense in which Christ receives His people from the Father's hand in time as well as in eternity. The text speaks of both the sovereignty of God and the responsibility of man and you cannot pare one down at the expense of the other, or stress one to the detriment of the other. C. H. Spurgeon, the great Baptist preacher of last century, was once asked, 'How do you reconcile free will and election?' and his reply was classic. He said, 'I never try to reconcile friends.' We long to see souls being saved in their hundreds and thousands throughout our land, but what a comfort it is to a faithful preacher of the gospel and to a praying congregation to believe and to know that there are those who will and who must and who shall be saved by the grace of God. If Christ has become precious to your soul, then be assured of this, that it was because God the Father took delight in you and gave you to the Son in the effectual donation of His grace. It was all of grace, all of God and nothing of you or me.

Secondly we have in this verse *The Approach of the Sinner,* - All that the Father giveth Me shall *come* to me. The action of God does not exclude the part that man has to play. Along with the action of God there is the activity of the person that is given. Jesus says, 'shall *come* to Me,' not 'shall *be brought* to Me,' expressing the activity of that person. The question arises: what does it mean to come to Christ? It means this, among many other things, to turn away from your sinful habits and ways. Let the wicked forsake his ways, and the unrighteous man his thoughts. These are the fruits of repentance. If repentance has taken place in the heart and soul, then there will be the evidence of it in the forsaking of evil and the putting away of sin. The Word of God calls us all to put away sin from us. Coming to Christ is also to trust in Him and in the sacrifice that He offered up on the Cross. Trust in Him alone for your salvation. Look to the blood that was shed there on the Cross for your salvation, saying, 'Lord, if I am going to be saved, I will only be saved by Your precious blood shed there on the Cross', believing that it was for you that He hung and suffered there.

Notice also the certainty of the fact that is stressed here - All that the Father hath given me *shall* come to Me. Every soul that God the Father gave to the Son shall come. It is a spiritual impossibility for them not to come. The Reformers stressed the doctrine of Irresistible Grace, and how right they were. There's no maybe, there's no perhaps about this. Jesus Himself said they shall come. It does not say that the person merely has the opportunity to come, or that in all probability he may come, but that he shall come. There is a ring of definite, absolute certainty about it and by this those that were secretly chosen by God are made known in this world when they openly choose Christ for themselves. They choose Christ for themselves because the Father has secretly chosen them first.

On the other hand it is also true that the person who continues in sin and in disobedience indicates that he is not one of Christ's sheep. That is a very solemn word for you if you are living in disobedience to the Word of God and going on in sin without caring about what God is saying to you. After hearing the gospel for many years you ought to ask yourself, 'Why am I not a Christian? Is it because I am not among those that Christ is going to call?' Jesus said that His sheep hear His voice and respond to His call. We are called to preach the gospel to every creature in the world. Jesus said to the disciples as He sent them out, 'Go ye into all the world and preach the gospel to every creature.' This is the means that God has ordained for souls to be saved and for His people to be brought in. The apostle Paul recognised this in 1 Corinthians 1 :21: 'It pleased God by the foolishness of preaching to save them that believe.' Bishop Ryle said that preaching is the hand of God by which He grasps those He has chosen to be saved from all eternity. Not only has our God chosen a people for Himself but He has chosen the means through which they are going to come in. We cannot tell them from others for they are scattered on the hillsides of time. We do not know who they are until they respond to the gospel and give evidence that they are listening and obeying the voice of the Shepherd.

There are those who are the sheep of Christ and are giving evidence of that very fact by their lives for they are walking in obedience to God. There are others and they are not yet walking in obedience to God but they are the sheep of God and they will come in yet, one day. Oh yes, they will come. But there are others, sadly, and they are in our cities, towns and villages, who will never come in and they will never be saved. They will never be converted because they are not the sheep of Christ. They were not given to the Son by the Father and they are lost. They are lost while they are living in this world. They are living and working, but they are lost and they will die in their sins. Jesus said to the Jews, 'You shall die in your sins and where I am ye cannot come.' But those that are Christ's, that He has earmarked from all eternity, might go on for thirty, forty, fifty, sixty and more years in disobedience. Yet before they die, they are going to be called effectually and savingly into the Kingdom and they are going to cry with the Philippian jailor, 'What must I do to be saved?' Has that cry ever risen from your heart?

There are none of them going to be left. Will you notice: *All* that the Father hath given Me. Not some, not part, but all! 'They shall be Mine,' sayeth the Lord, 'in that day when I make up my jewels.' But perhaps someone is saying that God is not fair when He deals with people like that. What is that person pleading for? He is pleading for justice. If God dealt with us in justice, the whole human race would be cast into a lost eternity with the devil and his angels. If it is justice you want, that is what you would get because that is what we deserve. But in mercy and in grace God has of His own free will chosen some and He has chosen to bypass others. Who are we to complain or find fault with God because He does that? You go into a shop and you look through the rack of suits or clothing and you choose a suit that you want. You go into the garage and you get a car but you bypass some garages when you choose that car. You chose your wife or you chose your husband. Why should we get angry with God because He chose a people for Himself to be with Him throughout eternity?

Thirdly, *The Reception by the Saviour* that Jesus Christ gives to the repentant sinner that comes to Him. Notice how personal this is, *him* that cometh to Me, not, *they* that come to Me. No! It's *him*, because as sinners we have personal needs, therefore we need a personal salvation. We need to meet with Christ personally in our own lives. God does not save people in groups. God saves men and women and boys and girls individually. Individually! There might be three, four, five people converted in one service but God deals with every one of them individually as if there was no one else in the world but them. We must come to the Saviour personally if we are to be saved. No one else can come for us. You cannot send your wife or your husband, or your father or mother, or sister or brother, or son or daughter in your place. *You* must come.

And then there is the word, *cometh*. It does not say how you are to come as long as you come. The point of it all is where you are to come to. It is to Jesus Christ, the Lamb of God crucified for sinners, that we are to come. There is no other name given among men under heaven whereby we can be saved but the name of Jesus. The angel said, 'Thou shalt call His name, Jesus, for He shall save His people from their sins' (Matthew 1:21).

It is not to the sacrament of baptism you are asked to come. That will not avail you anything. You are not asked to come to the church because the church will not save you. You are not asked to come to the Lord's table for salvation. The verse says, 'Come to Me' to

Jesus.

In this text there are the doctrines of God's Sovereignty, Election, Effectual Calling and Irresistible Grace but there is also here the necessity of faith. Those who are saved are saved only when they come to Jesus Christ in repentance and faith. He is the door into the sheepfold. There is no other way. Morality will not save you, your good works will not save you, your self righteousness will not save you; only the substitutionary sacrifice and atonement of Calvary's Cross will save you. In Him alone there is salvation and you do not need anything else apart from Christ. You do not need to go to a priest for salvation, you don't need to go to a minister for salvation, because they cannot even save themselves. It is Christ you need, not anyone else. 'Him that cometh to *Me*.' The woman with the issue of blood that the Bible speaks about said in her heart, 'If I but touch the hem of His garment.' She did not say, 'If I touch the hem of Peter's garment or John's garment I shall be healed.' We need to come to Him in repentance, weeping for our sins, and seeking for forgiveness. If you rest short of Christ, you rest short of the promise of this verse. Build your hopes on nothing less than the blood of Jesus and His righteousness.

Notice the certainty of the promise that Jesus gives here, 'I will in *no wise* cast him out', whether he be young, old, rich, or poor. Let him be morally upright or a reprobate, if he comes to Jesus, he will not be cast out. And He uses a double negative (in the Greek) for this. He says, in no wise, meaning, *not at all or never, by no means, never, ever* will I cast him out, if he comes to Me. It would violate all the divine properties of God if the Son was to refuse any of those that the

Father gave to Him. Would you refuse something that your father gave to you as a gift? No! You would never think of it, and the Son will not refuse those the Father gave to Him either. This means not only their reception at the beginning but also His never-failing and never ending embrace of them. There will never come the time when God the Son will put away from Him those that the Father gave to Him. They shall never perish, and neither shall any man pluck them out of His hand. They are dear to Him, they are precious to Him and He will in no wise cast them out. The gates of salvation are flung open for us here as wide as they can. Those who will be lost will be lost because of their sin and disobedience. There are those who respond to the gospel after hearing it for a short time. There are others who respond to the gospel after many, many years of sitting under the preaching of the Word of God. But Jesus says if they come to Him, He will in no wise cast them out. He will not hold it against them that they only heard the gospel once or twice. He will not hold it against them because they have sat for years listening to it. If they come to Him He will in no wise cast them out.

Some come in their early years while they are still at school. We are delighted to see this happening in Stornoway in these days. We see school-children coming to know Christ as their personal Saviour and going on with the Lord. There are others who are saved later on in life. Most of their lives have been spent in sin and in idleness and they are near to the gates of eternity. Then by the grace of God they turn to Christ for salvation and He says, 'I will in no wise cast them out. I am not going to cast them away if they turn to Me in the very last hour, as the thief on the cross did.' None of them are cast out. There are those who come with prayers and with tears in their eyes; there are others who come and they have no prayer at all, they cannot pray. There is only the groanings of their hearts and their conviction of sin. They do not know how to pray, they only cry and groan, but the Saviour says it doesn't matter, you don't need a long prayer for you to be accepted by Me. Oh, the groanings of the heart are sufficient.

This verse assures you that Christ will accept you if you come, whatever your condition. If you fall down at His mercy seat in repentance, seeking His pardon, believing that He died for you on the Cross, then with the hymnwriter we can say to you, 'None can perish there.' Approach the throne, approach the mercy seat, young or old, rich or poor, whatever your condition; for none can perish there if they come in the right spirit.

Those that will finally be lost will acknowledge that they are lost because of their own sin and disobedience to God. It is not God's fault. We are lost because we refused to listen to the gospel and refused the invitations of the Word of God. The fault lies with man and not with God. God never made man to sin.

Is someone saying that God will reject me because I have refused the offer of salvation so often down the years, or perhaps, I cannot pray properly so God will not accept me? He will! Those three little words ought to shatter any doubt or any fear that may be creeping into your heart, *in no wise*. In no wise, will God cast you out. We trust our friends, don't we, when they say that they will do something for us? We believe them and we accept their word. We accept the medicine that the doctor gives us without question and without doubt. Can we not accept the word of Jesus Christ when He says to us He will in no wise cast you out if you come in prayer, repenting of your sins? Why do we doubt the word of the Saviour when we take the word of men and act upon it?

Until the last soul is saved this word will stand true. No one will be cast out. Oh! you say, 'I have not got a broken heart. I do not feel the burden of my sins the way I should.' Well, listen to the words of Peter as he addressed another congregation many, many years ago in Acts 5:31. Speaking of Jesus, Peter says this, 'Him hath God exalted to His right hand to be a Prince and a Saviour, for to give repentance to Israel, and forgiveness of sins.' Ask Him for the grace that you feel you need. You say you cannot repent; then pray and ask God for the grace of repentance. You say that you cannot feel the burden of your sins; then ask God to show you something of what you are as a sinner. Ask God to show you yourself. Look at your past. Remember what kind of life you have lived. Oh, it's not a life of gross immorality or anything like deep sin! It's a life, I'm sure for most people, of forgetfulness of God, a life of selfishness. You have left God out of your life. It's not that you had gone deeply into sin in the past, that's not the most terrible thing about you, but that you have lived your life in forgetfulness of God, pleasing yourself instead of glorifying Him and living for Him. Ask God to melt down your hard heart. He is able to do it.

Ah! But you are saying that if you become a Christian, you cannot keep it up. You're right there - you cannot keep it up, but God can. He is able! He has kept everyone of us who profess Him. He has kept us and He will keep us till the river rolls its waters at our feet, then He will bear us gently over, made by grace for glory meet. Our strength is not in ourselves but in Him.

When do you expect then to come to Christ for salvation, repenting of your sins? Next year? In twenty years time? God says that today is the day of salvation. Now, at this very moment. You are not guaranteed another second more than you have got. Eternity is as near to us as that. You could die right where you are sitting just now and your opportunities would be gone for ever and you would enter into eternity. God says, 'He that cometh unto Me (now) I will in no wise cast out.'

I'm sure if you went down to hell tonight and if you opened the gates there and asked those that are there suffering in torment, you would find there would be those who would say to you: 'I was like that, and I promised myself that I would trust in Jesus Christ at a certain time in the future, but death came before that time and I'm here, and I am going to be here for ever and ever.'

Professor John Murray in one of his books says: 'It is on the crest of the wave of God's Sovereign Grace that the free overtures of the gospel break upon the shores of lost humanity.' They have come to you, the overtures of the gospel, of free grace, on the crest of the wave of God's Sovereignty in this service. What are you going to do with those overtures? Are you going to go out again, trampling under foot the blood of the Son of God?

We have looked at - 1. The Gift of the Father; 2. The Approach of the Sinner; and 3. The Reception by the Saviour.

There is a story told about a ship that was lost in

117

fog at sea long before there were any of the modern navigational aids that are at the disposal of sailors in our day. This ship sailed up the Amazon River quite unaware that it was the Amazon. They had been for many days without water and were dying of thirst. Then they saw a ship coming towards them and sent out a message, 'Give us water, we are dying.' This was the reply that came back, 'Dip it up, Dip it up!' They were sailing in fresh water and they were dying of thirst, yet they were unaware of where they were! The rivers of God's grace and mercy are flowing through this gathering and there are some dying of thirst in it. Dip it up right where you are! May God bless unto us the preaching of His Word.

1988

Professor Edward Donnelly,
Reformed Presbyterian Church of Ireland

Repentance (Luke 15 v.18)

I will arise and go to my father, and will say to him,
'Father, I have sinned against heaven and before you.'

I would like to speak to you this evening from the
parable of the Prodigal Son on the subject of
Repentance. Repentance seems, I suppose, an
old-fashioned word to many people today. At any
rate, it is not heard as frequently as it once was. For
some it may conjure up pictures of mediaeval
disciplines, of monks torturing their bodies or
engaging in strange, ascetic practices. Others think,
perhaps, of the penitents' bench of past centuries.
The most common view is that repentance is
something appropriate for the most wretched and
degraded of humanity but not really for the ordinary
man or woman. It is considered unusual,
extraordinary, out of the common run of experience.
Yet, when we look at the Scriptures, we see how
fundamental repentance is to our relationship with
God and to the whole of the Christian life.

The importance of repentance is stressed in many
places throughout the Bible. If we were to ask, for
example, what was one of the chief reasons why our
Lord came to earth, we would find the answer in Luke
5:32, where He says, 'I have not come to call the
righteous, but sinners, to repentance.' The coming of
the Saviour is inextricably linked with the call to
repentance. Or we might think of the resurrection of

Christ. He is now raised from the dead and exalted to the right hand of God. What was the purpose of such exaltation? Acts 5:31 tells us: 'Him God has exalted to His right hand to be Prince and Saviour, to give repentance to Israel and forgiveness of sins.' One of the great purposes of the exaltation and enthronement of Christ is that He might give repentance to men and women.

In Acts 17:30 we find the apostle Paul saying that, 'God now commands all men everywhere to repent.' Here, in other words, is a commandment which is truly universal, addressed to all people in every age and every country. Every member of the human race, without exception, is summoned to repentance by the Lord. Again, we might think of heaven and of the great joy and happiness of that place. The redeemed are in the presence of God and the angels surround His throne. What is it which causes joy in heaven, which calls forth songs of praise and exclamations of worship? Christ Himself answers that there is joy in heaven over one sinner who repents (Luke 15:7).

Repentance is God's universal command. It is the only alternative to perishing. It is that which causes joy in heaven. It is fundamental to the Christian life. We shall look at the subject of repentance from the words we read: 'I will arise and go to my father, and will say to him, "Father, I have sinned against heaven and before you." ' We are going to take from the verse three statements by the Prodigal Son, because repentance has never been more clearly and brilliantly illustrated than in this parable. As we think of this subject, we should each one be asking ourselves, 'Am I repentant? Is it part of my daily experience? Could I be described as a penitent man or woman, a penitent boy or girl?' Here are three elements of true repentance.

We find in the first place that the prodigal realised his sin. *I have sinned!* Those three short words take very little time to say and yet what a world of meaning they contain! What a transformation in his thinking has brought him to speak thus! What a mighty work of God has taken place in this man's heart and life to bring him to the point where he can say and mean, 'I have sinned!' He realised his sin.

He would not have spoken these words at the beginning of the story. He was a young man, eager to sample life and all that it promised. He was impatient of the restrictions of home. He regarded his father perhaps as someone who was keeping him tied down, holding him back from all that life had to offer. Most young people want to break loose and be free. He wanted to make his own way in the world. He wanted to discover life for himself, to experience it to the full, and as he left his father's home that day, he had no sense of wrongdoing, no feeling that he was breaking any commandment. He went, I am sure, with a light step and a lighter heart. The whole world was his oyster. He looked forward to unlocking its adventures and challenges. What was wrong with that? He had no sense of sin at that point.

He would not have spoken these words as he arrived in the far country and plunged enthusiastically into its lifestyle. If we had been able to question him and ask, 'What is your opinion of the life which you are leading?', he would have answered, 'I am just doing what everyone else is doing. I am no worse than others. We have money and youth and energy and we are using them to enjoy ourselves. I am having a wonderful time.' There was no sense of sin then.

He would not have spoken these words just after his money was gone, and all his friends had deserted him and he was forced to beg for degrading work, feeding pigs. He was miserable and unhappy but he still had no sense of sin. Perhaps he would have admitted that he had been foolish and naive. He might confess to have made many mistakes in life and taken a wrong turning, and was now paying for it. But he still had no sense of sin. It is only when he says, 'I have sinned,' that we understand that something deeper has gripped him, a new dimension has entered his thinking. He sees his past in a new light, in its full horror of selfishness and ingratitude.

Think for a moment! Here is a young man who owes everything to his father. His father has given him life, fed him, clothed him, provided for him, trained him, disciplined him and loved him. His father has shown kindness and patience. But how has this son treated his father? He has taken and taken and taken but has given nothing. He has not loved his father, he has not honoured or trusted him. He said, 'Father, give me the portion of goods that falls to me.' What he was really saying was, 'My only interest in you, father, is in the cash which I will get when you are dead - and I can't wait until you actually drop dead, so could I please have it now?'

Can you imagine what those words meant to his father? He did not want to live in his father's presence. He did not want to talk to him or listen to him or confide in him. He takes everything from his father, gives nothing in return and then repudiates the relationship. Now, as he thinks of what he has done, he sees how shameless and heartless he has been. His sin was not the harlots or the wasting of the money or the far country. It began farther back than that. His sin was a failure to love, a failure to serve, a failure to render to his father that duty which he owed him. These other things, these ugly, obvious sins, which we would all condemn, were only manifestations of a heart that was cold and dead and ungrateful. As he reflects, it is that which wounds him and breaks him and leads him to cry out in agony, 'Father, I have sinned against heaven and before you.' He realised his sin.

How many prodigals are here this evening? I'm not talking about the great, glaring, black sins which would call forth the condemnation of all right-thinking people. We may look at ourselves and say, 'My life is free of such things. I am not a drunkard or a wife-beater. I am not a thief.' Such wrongdoing may not be present in our lives, but what about the God who made you, who gave you life, who at this very moment holds you in His hand? All that you have and all that you are is from Him. The very breath that you are now drawing in through your nostrils is His gift. He is your Creator and Preserver and you owe much to Him. You owe Him love and gratitude, service and obedience and worship.

The beginning of sin is godlessness, ingratitude, a failure to bow down, a failure to give thanks; and there are many people, perhaps many here, who are upright, moral, respectable and kindly - but godless. Do you serve your God in worship and praise and humble gratitude? If you do not, that is of the very essence of sin - not to glorify God, not to be thankful. So often we insulate ourselves from conviction. We draw up a list of actions and we say, 'These are sins, but I do not do these things, therefore I am not guilty.' But Christ here teaches that not to love the Father, not to serve the Father, not to acknowledge your indebtedness to Him - that is sin. This is what it means to be a prodigal. It is really saying to God, 'Give me all the gifts I want, and then, as far as I am concerned, You might as well be dead.' Are you someone for whom God might as well be dead? What difference would it make to your life if God no longer existed? You rarely read His Word. You spend only a few moments at best seeking Him in prayer. You know little of what it means to serve, obey, worship and love Him. You do not recognise your indebtedness to Him. Christ is here teaching us, perceptively and penetratingly, what sin is and how all the other uglinesses spring from that evil root.

What about those who are true Christians? It is easy for one to say, 'I have repented,' but repentance is to be the daily practice of the Christian. How easy it is to take and not to give! How often we do it! But sin is not abstract or impersonal. Sin is not a matter of transgressing some concept or theory. Sin is shaking our fist at a loving, gracious God. Would you treat your father or mother the way this prodigal treated his father? Would you not be ashamed to do it? Yet, are you treating God that way? We have to feel the bitter shame and scalding contempt of a sense of sin. It is personal. Do you remember how David cried out, 'Against You, You only, have I sinned, and done this evil in Your sight?' (Psalm 51:4). God has given us all, but what have we given Him? I have sinned.

We see, in the second place, that the prodigal left the far country - *I will arise*. This man was sorrowful, he felt ashamed and guilty, but he did not stop with feelings. He did something. Many people think of repentance only in emotional terms as if to repent is only to feel sorry. Yes, it is to feel sorry, but it is more than that. J C Ryle puts it this way: 'Action is the very life of saving repentance.' Feelings, tears, remorse, wishes and resolutions are all useless until they are accompanied by action and a change of life. So, this young man not only says, 'I have sinned', but adds, '*I will arise.*' He comes to a momentous decision. He is going to change the whole course and perspective of his life. He is going to move in the opposite direction. He decides to leave his employment and acquaintances, to separate himself from his surroundings, to abandon the country in which he has been living. He turns his back on these things, he walks away from them. He separates himself decisively from that which he had loved and sought and worked for. He repudiates all the connections he had chosen and sets out on the long road home to make his confession.

We come close here to the core of repentance because when the Holy Spirit touches the hearts of sinners when He imparts to them that gift of repentance and when they see their sin as ingratitude and rebellion against a holy God, they then naturally separate themselves from that sin. This is the miraculous, supernatural element in repentance. 'Being sorry enough,' as the little boy said, 'to quit.' There is no repentance without it! It does not matter what we think or what we feel. We may have a very good intellectual grasp of what repentance means. We may weep rivers of tears. We may be able to describe our sorrow in graphic terms. But, if there is no radical change in our behaviour, then there has been no true repentance.

You cannot know God's blessing in the far country. The prodigal son could not send a letter home and say, 'Dear father, please send a cheque. I'm sorry for what I have done. I understand my mistakes now, and if you could see your way to making a monthly allowance, I will try to keep in touch.' He had to go home. We simply cannot experience God's blessing while we are practising sin. We cannot serve God effectively while practising sin. We cannot believe that we are in a saved condition while deliberately and consciously and willingly practising sin. We cannot even pray while practising sin: 'If I regard iniquity in my heart, the Lord will not hear' (Psalm 66:18). We cannot enjoy God and sin at the same time, and if we are repentant we are brought to the point where we say, 'I will arise, I will set out, I will leave these things.'

Are some of you unconverted? If you are to know salvation and eternal life, there must be a turning from godlessness, from self-centredness, from pride and self-will. You must say,' I will arise, I will set out, by God's help I will leave these things.'

What about the prayerless among us? Is God speaking to you about your neglect of prayer? You have read books on prayer, you know all the right things to say, but day after day in your life passes, and you are not on your knees in the presence of God, seeking His favour and blessing. Will you say, 'I will arise, I will set out, I will leave this thing?'

What about the self-centred? What, self-centred Christians? Yes, how easy it is for that poison to come back into the hearts of all of us! The self-centred preacher or elder, the self-centred Sabbath School teacher, the self-centred husband or wife, son or daughter - a covering of piety, but consumed by self-esteem. Will you say, 'I will arise, I will set out, I will leave this thing!'

Many other sins might be mentioned. You know your own weaknesses. But if anyone among you realises that, in whole or in part, you are in the far country of sin, and if you are resolving in your heart of hearts not to leave it, please do not deceive yourself. You are not repentant, you do not know what it means, and I tell you that, unless God has mercy on you, you will perish. The prodigal separated from his sin, he turned his back on it, and so must you.

Then, thirdly and lastly, he went back to his father. *I will arise and go to my father.* Why do you think he really left the far country? Why did he go home? He was disillusioned and disappointed with his life, but that is not why he went home. He was hungry and needy and poor, but that is not why he went home. He felt guilty and ashamed, but that is not why he went home. Something far stronger was working in this son's heart. As he sat there, conscious of his sin and desiring to be free from it, there arose in his mind the vision of his home, of his father's face and voice, and a wave of intense homesickness swept over him and the thought came into his mind, 'I believe my father would take me back.' Surely we Celts, Scots and Irish, can understand that. One of the pictures which is burnt into our national consciousness, in our songs and poetry, is the emigrant ship and the people at the dock leaving their native land, perhaps for ever. Homesickness is the burden of the wanderer. Many of us know what it is, in strange places of the world, to think back to home, to our father and mother. This son, in his need, suddenly thought of the good and loving face of his father and, overwhelmed by that awareness, cried out, 'I want to go home.' That is the beauty of the gospel. When I speak to you of repentance, I am not speaking of some grim, dogged work of reformation. I am not speaking simply of realisation of sin and turning from sin; I am speaking also about going home.

Do you remember the definition of the Shorter Catechism? 'Repentance unto life is a saving grace, whereby a sinner, out of a true sense of his sin, and' .... What?....'apprehension of the mercy of God in Christ.' The repentant man or woman apprehends or grasps God's mercy, and then, ..'doth, with grief and hatred of his sin, turn from it unto God'. Repentance is not just about leaving the far country, repentance is about going home. Repentance is not just about forsaking sin, repentance is finding the Father. And the purpose of repentance for this young man was not just to lead him to sever his sinful relationships: that was merely a means to an end. The true purpose was to restore his relationship with his father. The whole point was to bring him home.

In repentance we realise our sin, and that is important. In repentance we resolve to leave our sin, and that is also important. But what is most vital of all is that the Holy Spirit brings home to our hearts that the Lord is a merciful, loving and gracious God, and that He has sent His Son, the Lord Jesus Christ, to bear in His body the sins of His people. Now there is forgiveness with God that He may be feared, and the sinner may cry to Him for mercy, and through Christ, such mercy will be given. The prodigal came to believe that, if he went and sought mercy from his father, his father would receive him, and it was that belief which finally brought him home.

I could speak to you more about sin, and seek, by the help of the Holy Spirit, to wound your consciences. Our sin is desperately foul and ugly and we must be done with it. But I want to stress even more that the Saviour, the Lord Jesus Christ, has come and has lived a perfect life for His people, and has paid the price of their sins when He died for them. If you will come to Him and ask Him to forgive you and to cleanse you, He will do it. His promise is that, 'The one who comes to me I will by no means cast out' (John 6:37). Repentance is not just a turning from sin, though it is that. It is a turning to God.

God speaks to us now, to you and to me, for, like you, I too have sinned this day against my God. Can we each say, 'I have sinned?' Can we each say, by God's gracious help and mercy, 'I will arise, I will leave my sin?' Can we each say, 'I will go to my Father and I will ask Him, for the sake of His dear Son, to receive me and to forgive me. I will trust Christ for my salvation?'

Jesus once stood and called to a dead man, 'Lazarus, come forth!' (John 11:43). Just as there was power in that call to awaken the dead, so now, in my Master's name, I call you to repent, to say, 'I have sinned, I will arise, I will go to my Father,' and, as Spurgeon said, 'if we limp towards Him, He will run towards us.'

And he arose and came to his father. But when he was still a great way off, his father saw him and had compassion, and ran and fell on his neck and kissed him. May there be joy in heaven tonight. Amen!

1989

Professor Donald MacLeod,
Free Church College, Edinburgh

Justify the Ungodly (Romans 4 v 5)

My thanks for your very warm welcome. I want to focus on words of Paul's Epistle to the Romans chapter 4 verse 5 and this phrase in particular, *Him who justifies the ungodly.* I was asked to focus tonight on one of the central tenets of the Christian gospel and to bring fundamental Bible truth to bear upon the needs of those gathered before me. And I turn mindful of that to this great doctrine of Justification and I do so for several reasons.

First, it is by any standard one of the great foundation truths of the New Testament. It lies at the very core of the gospel, in fact *is* the core of the gospel. I turn to it also because its rediscovery away back in the 16th Century by Martin Luther liberated the soul of Europe and gave the impetus to the emergence of civilisation as we know it today. It is impossible to overestimate the impact which this discovery had, the sense of emancipation, of exhilaration, of peace with God which freed man's creativity for the great ventures in modern science, politics and culture.

I turn to it too because I think it does bear so directly upon our own emotional state, upon the way that we feel. I have observed, and sometimes at very close quarters, the problem of spiritual depression in many of its phases and I am more and more convinced that that spiritual despondency is most often the consequence of a lack of understanding of the terms on which God deals with man. I believe that a real tenacious and clear grasp of this mighty truth will provide a stable foundation for a sense of peace with God and for joy and contentment in the citadel of our own souls. And so it stands before us as a great foundational truth, it stands before us as a truth of great historic moment and consequence and it stands before us as a truth which matters so much to our own peace and to our own contentment.

But I turn to it above all because it is God's answer to sin. I address an audience expert on crime; not, you will note, expert *in* crime but expert *on* crime. Crime is the violation of man's law. It is outward, visible, palpable, demonstrable and provable. All crime is sin, but there is sin which is not crime. Sin is violation of God's law. I am not going to accuse you of sin. I may put it to you this way, that I speak as a sinner. I remember the great words of Thomas Chalmers, 'What would I do , were it not that God justifies the ungodly?' I believe that my life is by God's standards indefensible because if I measure the way I live by God's imperatives, by God's demand that I love my neighbour as myself, that I love God with my whole heart and soul, then by those standards my life is indefensible.

I'm going to be so bold as to insinuate that your lives too are indefensible, that the upholders of the law are themselves breakers of the law. I'm going to suppose that you, too, know that in your lives there is lovelessness and there is self-indulgence. In your lives there is so much that is anarchic, that is selfish, that is egotistical, that is disruptive, that is destructive. I'm going to insinuate that sometimes you fall short of the great standards of your own esteemed profession. I'm going to suggest that sometimes you, too, cause pain and sometimes you, too, disappoint. I am assuming that you are sinners and I have to say that if you are not a sinner then you can indeed switch off because this whole message of God, this whole Christian faith, is God's word directed to sin, and God has nothing to say to the righteous, God has no word for the perfect. He has no word for those who regard their lives as completely defensible. But I am going to suppose that you are sinners.

I will also remind you that one day you will stand before God and give an account, just as I shall, at the great Assize, conducted by the omniscient Judge. I believe it will be the fairest court of law ever convened. God will listen to every plea you offer in mitigation, to every word of explanation. You can come with all the arguments of the psychologists and the sociologists and the geneticists and the criminologists, and you can explain to God all the reasons in your background and your heredity and your environment, all those factors that explain or mitigate the way you have been, and you will receive the most marvellous hearing. It will be meticulously fair but I promise you that at the end of God's examination that every mouth will be stopped and the whole world will be guilty before God.

Not only are you a sinner but you *know* you are a sinner. Not only will you one day stand before God as Judge but you *know* that one day you will stand before God as Judge. We can do what we like with our consciences - we can stifle them, pamper them, educate them, sophisticate them, and we can try to bluff them, but our consciences will come and say to us, 'Look, this is the truth - you are a sinner and one day you will stand before the Throne of God.' And it's into that great fact, into that great fact of conscience, into what you know about yourself, that I want tonight to preach this great truth, *God justifies the ungodly*.

Let me put it to you in the most provocative way I can. Who is the man that God justifies? What kind of man do you need to be to be right with God? What a tremendous truth it is that you can be an ungodly man or woman and yet in the mystery of God's grace, you can be right with God even though you have been ungodly!

Let us examine this great truth for a moment. What does it mean when it says that God justifies? What does He do when He engages in this particular act? It means that God forgives all our sins, that He completely cancels all the guilt that stands against us. I am not going to tell you what your record is, but you know the areas where your life has been indefensible. I would remind you that when God justifies a man or a woman He completely eradicates and erases all that stands in the debit against them. This great truth Paul put this way, 'There is no condemnation to them that are in Christ Jesus.'

Let me put it to you this way. In almost every human life there is that one great sin. There is something in your past that rises up and torments you. It accuses you, and your conscience asks whenever you think of God and of peace with Him, 'How can you think of peace with God? Remember that one sin?' I believe that all the dialecticians and rhetoricians of hell love to get men and women bogged down in this great pit, this one sin, this something of which we are so profoundly ashamed. We see it standing between ourselves and God until the New Testament says this to us that, 'The blood of Jesus Christ, God's Son, cleanses from all sin.' Tonight I want you to take the greatest sin in your life and I want you to look it straight in the eyes. I want you to examine it in all its horror, all its ugliness and all its vileness and I want you to say to yourself, 'the blood of Jesus Christ, God's Son, cleanses from all sin.' This means it cleanses from this one sin which tonight stands between you and peace.

Let me put it to you another way. Do you know, the marvel of God's gospel is that at last you can be as righteous as Christ, as righteous as God Himself. There is no condemnation! I have tonight, conscious of all my own personal failings, to believe that God has nothing against me, that God accepts me as I am, that God has cancelled the past, that God has forgiven all the sin, all that's twisted, all that's arrogant, all that's egotistical, all that's violent - God has forgiven it and that I have no stain or guilt. That is the Rock on which I stand. It means that God forgave all my sin.

I'll put it another way. It means that God accepts us. You imagine again this court of law. There is the Judge on the bench, there is the accused in the dock, and yet God acquits and forgives. God says there is no condemnation, and that surely is a great truth. But God goes on to say that the law has nothing against you. It is as if you had never sinned. The slate is wiped completely clean and you are accepted with God. What do I mean? It means that the Judge takes you into His own family. He does not simply say to the prisoner, 'You are free to go.' He does not simply leave him to walk the streets, maybe jobless, maybe homeless, maybe penniless, but He makes him His own child. He gives us all the rights of members of His own family. He makes us heirs of God and joint-heirs with Jesus Christ. It is not only a question of all our sin being forgiven. It is this astonishing and remarkable transformation that God takes me into His own home, into His own family and says, 'All I have is yours!' I said a moment ago that we are as righteous as Christ. I want you to believe this, that if you know the grace and privilege of Justification, then you are as rich as Christ, since you are an heir of God. In the family of God, all are firstborn sons and have the rights of primogeniture, of every blessing, every privilege, every resource that God has.

One of the great problems that we have in our world today, often unsuspected, is the difficulty people have accepting themselves. The profound discontent that people have with their own body shapes, with their own personality, with the colour of their own skin, with their own achievement, causes the constant pressure towards self-disparagement and self-loathing. One of the great things that we have in Justification which meant so much to Martin Luther is that it teaches me that God accepts me as I am. Woody Allen, if I may quote such an authority, said once, 'My one regret in life is that I'm not somebody else,' and that is the problem with so many people. That is our great regret, that we are not somebody else, until we come to experience the glory of this, that God accepts us as we are. He knows the truth about you and me, and still He forgives, still He accepts, still He loves. I believe that the anchor in the storms of life is to know that we are right with God who will never let us go and who can never make any discovery that will cause Him to change His mind. He accepts me as I am, and what peace and what emancipation there is in that mighty fact!

But then I ask this. On what ground and for what reason does God accept us, forgive our sins and make us members of His own family? This was the great problem that Luther faced, 'How could a man be right with God?' He became a monk, in a very strict Order, lived a most austere life, trying every possible form of penance, self-punishment and spiritual exercise. Yet he said at the end of it all, 'If any man could have got to heaven by monkery then I would have got to heaven,' because he had put so much of his own personal effort into earning his own salvation. And that is the problem! We want to walk into heaven with our heads high. We want to walk into heaven as self-made men and say, 'Look, Lord, I saved myself, and I am coming on the basis of my own achievement.' The gospel often puts this whole marvellous truth in terms of negatives - the things you do not need to do, and the kind of person you do not have to be, in order to be right with God. What I need is a justification for the ungodly because that is what I am, and I am so impolite as to imagine and to insinuate that that's what you need also - a justification for the ungodly; and that is why this gospel, to a large extent consists of those great negatives, of the things you do not need to have to be right with God. Let me share them with you.

It is not by *works,* it is not what we do. We do not have to climb great mountains, to endure great pain, to bear great burdens, overcome great temptations or great privations. The man who has nothing of which he can boast can still be right with God. St Bernard said, 'My problem is not that I cannot answer for my sins but that I cannot answer for my righteousness.' There may be some here perceptive enough to know that they have nothing that they can bring to God. Are you prepared to go to God and say, 'Lord, this is a sinner speaking, this is an ungodly man. I have nothing to bring, I have nothing to boast of?' Have you the faith tonight to go to God on those terms, to believe that your standing before God is not a matter of being good or of doing good? Your standing before God does not depend on what kind of day you have had. What we do is a great irrelevance as far as our acceptance with God is concerned

Or again, put it this way. It does not depend on our *own religious experience*. The Reformers had this great doctrine that Justification does not depend on grace within us. That is why so often Christians are in such terrible trouble. They are depressed and confused because they look at their experience. Bear with me on this for a moment. Their conviction of sin is very poor. Their love for the brethren is very poor. Their hunger and thirsting for God, His Word and righteousness is very poor. What are they doing? They are looking at their *experience* and that is why I said that so much depression is the direct result of not grasping this doctrine. The great problem is that we are looking to our experiences, to what we feel, to what happens in our own lives, to our own graces. Are we meek? Are we merciful? Are we patient and longsuffering? And the devil comes along and says, 'Well, look! Look at that meekness! See the cracks, see the flaws? Not up to much, is it? Can you stand on that? Can you go to God on the basis of those experiences?' You say, 'No, devil, certainly not!' And there, before you know it, you are again spiralling downwards into this morass, into this darkness, because you are all confused and all wrong. We imagine that our standing before God depends on our own feelings and experiences. If I can just dare quote a few great words of Gaelic Hymnody, from John MacDonald of Ferintosh. Doctor Chalmers, if I can digress for a moment, was once asked, 'What is MacDonald's secret? Why is it that wherever that man goes there is such mighty spiritual power?' Chalmers said, 'I know his secret. He preaches Justification by Faith Alone.' MacDonald put it this way,

Na rinn 's na dh'fhuiling Slànuighear
ar sud an aìt a shluaigh,
'S e sud a's bunait teàrnaidh dhomh,
'S cha'n e gach gràs a fhuair.

What a Saviour did and suffered,
In His people's room and stead,
That's the ground of my salvation,
Not any grace conferred.

It is not a question of inward experience, precious though that is. That is not the rock on which we stand. God has put our feet on a Rock, and that Rock is not the rock of experience or the rock of gifts or the rock of graces. And I want you to be able to go to God and say, 'Lord, my gifts are few, my grace is weak and yet Lord, I have peace with you, because my standing does not depend on what I do and it does not depend on what I experience.'

The Reformers put a third negative in when they said this, 'Do not look to faith as the ground of your salvation.' Now, faith is enormously important. Another great Scottish teacher, 'Rabbi' John Duncan, put it this way. He asked a great question which I want you to remember. He asked, 'Was faith crucified for you? Was it faith that went to the Cross?' Look at that faith, - up one day and down the next. Call that a rock?

I remember hearing once of an open air preacher who was being heckled by a gentleman of Irish extraction, and to everything the preacher said, this Irishman shouted, *Shamrock!* Whatever the preacher said there was the refrain, Shamrock! At last the preacher quoted these great words, 'On Christ, the solid Rock I stand, all other ground is ..... SHAM ROCK.' I believe there are many Christians standing often on SHAM rock - on the rock of graces, on the rock of faith. Faith is not the Rock. Faith is your feet, is your standing, is your grasp of the Rock, is your grip, but it is not the Rock. The Rock does not move come wind, come weather. Ebb or flow, the Rock does not move. But does not our faith move? And if you are standing on that faith then many a day you will be spiritually sea-sick - up one day and down the next. Our faith is one of those things that needs forgiveness!

You, tonight, can have few works to your credit and still you can get right with God. You can be very unhappy with your own religious experience and still be right with God. And you can be very, very unhappy about your faith and still be right with God. Why? 'On Christ, the solid Rock I stand.' He is the ground of our salvation. How marvellously objective it is, outside of me, independent of me that on the Cross of Calvary, there Christ bore all my sins. He became what Luther called the greatest sinner that ever was, the most guilty person this world ever saw as He bore the guilt of His people. The Lamb of God bearing the sin of the world - what a great and familiar truth it is. I have never heard it put better than in the words of the black American Christian who said, 'Either He die or me die; He die, me no die!'

Do you realise as Christians, (if we are Christians,) that every single sin was borne by Christ, every sin we ever committed? What a great truth that is, but it is not the greatest truth. There is a greater truth, an incredible truth, that all the *righteousness of Christ* was made over to you, - this mighty fact that Christians are as righteous and as blameless and as free from guilt as Christ Himself. He bore *all my sins,* He made over to me *all His righteousness,* and I am righteous with all the righteousness that God can require. No wonder Luther felt such exhilaration. There he was vexed and tormented with this tremendous impulse towards self-salvation, and the harder he tried the more woeful his performance seemed to himself as he struggled to get right with God and slipped further and further into the morass, into the pit. Then he grasped this, that *Christ* was his righteousness. His name is Jehovah Tsidkenu - The Lord our Righteousness.

If you are a Christian, you are as righteous before God on the bad days as you are on the good days because it depends on Him, it depends on the Rock. Let me ask you this as I close. What kind of man does God justify? What kind of person does God accept? Well, you say to me, a good man, a good woman, a good boy or girl. No! He justifies the ungodly! That is the most dangerous truth a man can utter, and yet it is the truth. God accepts you as a sinner, not after you have dealt with sin and crucified sin and had it licked, but as we are.

'Just as I am, without one plea
But that Thy blood was shed for me

And that Thou bidst me come to Thee,
Oh Lamb of God I come.

Just as I am and waiting not,
To rid my soul of one dark spot,
But that Thy blood may cleanse each blot,
Oh Lamb of God I come!'

That is the great problem, you see. We want to cease being ungodly before we come to God, and I am saying to you in God's name, 'You must come to God as ungodly, as sinners, just as you are, without one plea.' You have not made progress, you say. Well God says, 'Come as you are!' Even though you have not made progress, even though you are still defeated by sin and have made no penance, come as an ungodly man. This is what the Bible is saying, 'He justifies the ungodly.'

But that cannot be the whole truth. No! He justifies the ungodly who *believe in Jesus.* We are God's righteousness in Him. That is the great question and challenge tonight. Are we in Christ? That is the one thing that matters. The great protection that this Doctrine has is that the only place in the world where you can be justified is in Christ, and if you are in Christ then, of course, you cannot live as you please because you are rooted in Him. The very point where God provides for our forgiveness, He provides for our transformation. He will change us through Christ, but I want to keep you to this one point. You need nothing but Christ. He can bear the whole weight of your salvation.

I plead with those of you tonight who are in Christ, who have faith no matter how weak. Will you please accept the glory of your condition and do not let your condition be modified and altered by moods and by your own performance, because at the end of the day that is not what matters. We are in Christ! A Saviour's obedience and blood hide all my transgressions from view. Do we believe that? It is the most difficult thing in the whole world to believe that the one factor that determines my standing before God is that I am in Christ. And I want every one of God's people here tonight to feel the glory and the exhilaration of this; we are in Christ and in a way nothing else matters. This is the one thing that determines how things are between your soul and God this evening.

But those of you who are not right with God, I tell you it really matters to be right with Him and I remind you that the only thing that matters, as far as putting that relationship right, is to be in Christ. I wonder tonight if I can persuade, through God's Word and in the power of His Spirit, any of you, all of you, to make that journey.

All the lawkeepers, and the law enforcement officers who are lawbreakers - who are God's lawbreakers - should be right with God. You can be right with God simply because there is one thing true of you, 'You are in Christ.' Do you stand on this solid Rock? May God grant it so.